IRELAND

THROUGH THE AGES

Art of the Celtic Revival in the chapel of University College, Cork.

IRELAND

THROUGH THE AGES

written and photographed by
MICHAEL JENNER

Also by Michael Jenner

YEMEN REDISCOVERED
BAHRAIN – GULF HERITAGE IN TRANSITION
SYRIA IN VIEW
SCOTLAND THROUGH THE AGES
LONDON HERITAGE
A TRAVELLER'S COMPANION TO THE WEST COUNTRY
JOURNEYS INTO MEDIEVAL ENGLAND

PENGUIN BOOKS
Published by the Penguin Group
Penguin Books Ltd, 27 Wrights Lane, London W8 5TZ, England
Penguin Books USA Inc., 375 Hudson Street, New York, New York 10014, USA
Penguin Books Australia Ltd, Ringwood, Victoria, Australia
Penguin Books Canada Ltd, 10 Alcorn Avenue, Toronto, Ontario, Canada M4V 3B2
Penguin Books (NZ) Ltd, 182–190 Wairau Road, Auckland 10, New Zealand

Penguin Books Ltd, Registered Offices, Harmondsworth, Middlesex, England

First Published in Great Britain in 1992 by Michael Joseph Ltd

This edition first published by
Claremont Books, an imprint of Godfrey Cave Associates Limited,
42 Bloomsbury Street, London WC1B 3QJ, 1996

ISBN 1 8547 1823 1

Printed in Italy

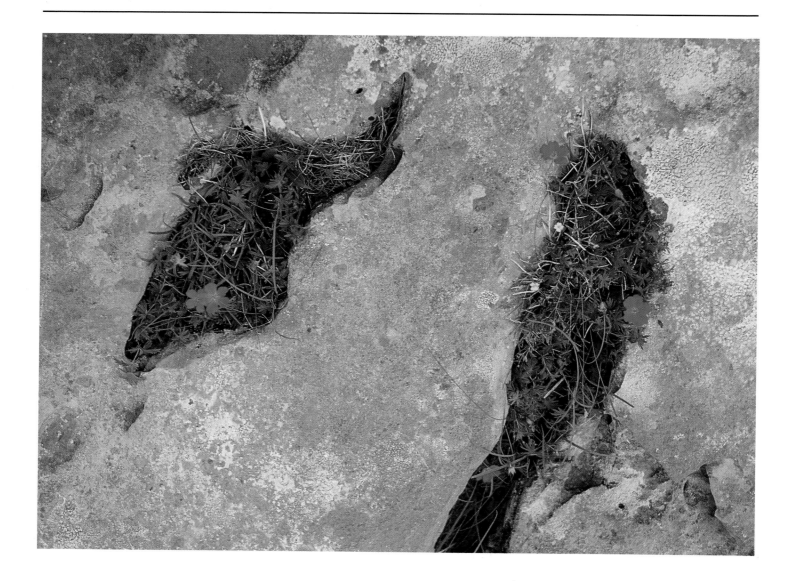

Wild flowers nestling in the crevices of a limestone pavement are characteristic of the Burren in County Clare.

CONTENTS

To the people of Ireland wherever they may be.

ACKNOWLEDGEMENTS

Travel and research the length and breadth of Ireland were generously facilitated by Bord Fáilte Eireann, the Northern Ireland Tourist Board, Shannon Development, Aer Lingus and Britannia Airways. Particular thanks are due to Mark Rowlette of the Irish Tourist Board in London who masterminded the main part of my Irish odyssey, and to his colleagues in Dublin, Ellen Redmond and Peter Harbison. Ian Hill, Rosemary Evans and Libby Kinney of the Northern Ireland Tourist Board were most helpful in pointing me in the right direction. In the course of my travels I met with kind assistance from a great number of people: Sylvia Brickenden of Cratloe Woods House, Paul Caffrey of Castletown, Mr C. D. Cholmeley-Harrison of Emo Court, Luke Dodd of Strokestown Park House, Diane Forbes of the National Trust for Northern Ireland, the Harringtons of Glencarne House, Manix and Sally Magee of Irvinestown, the Percevals of Temple House, Nicholas Prins of Lissadell, Des and Pat Lavelle of Valentia Island, the Marquess of Sligo, Tom and Eileen O'Connor, John Toolin at Kilmainham Gaol, Sam Scott of the Ulster Folk and Transport Museum, Rosemary and Eric White of Maddybenny Farm. In addition there are many other individuals, whose names have passed out of remembrance though their kindness is not forgotten, such as the ladies of Thoor Ballylee, Fota House and the Cashel Palace Hotel who revived me with refreshments and the companiable ferrypersons who took me to White Island in Lough Erne. I would also like to record my thanks to the owners and custodians of Dunkathel House, the Irish Agricultural Museum, the Nora Barnacle House in Galway and St Michan's Dublin in addition to all those at the many places illustrated in this book.

The dead slumber on undisturbed in this overgrown churchyard at Durrow, Co. Offaly: a haunting reminder of the past.

ONE FOOT IN THE PAST

IRELAND'S PAST is the inspiration behind this book, not because Irish people live in the past, rather that the past still lives in Ireland – and to an intense degree. The country bears the scars and trophies of its chequered destiny more visibly than most. History – tinged with bitter-sweet memories – wafts about in the very air you breathe and lurks quite physically too in a landscape that is liberally strewn with ancient monuments. History looms large in this book, but its role is that of a background against which to appreciate the country as it presents itself to the traveller of today. So this is intended not as yet another illustrated history of Ireland but more as an evocation of Ireland as interpreted through a multitude of historic places, which mark the main chapters of the Irish saga. The approach has been to follow the signposts provided by an amazing variety of relics and remains, so that archaeology and architecture are more prominently featured than the dates of events or the ambitions of personalities. Nevertheless, these aspects do bubble up to the surface throughout the narrative by virtue of their relevance to specific sites and monuments.

That the past is alive and well and living in Ireland, there can be no doubt. The most obvious sign of this is the traditional veneration of ancestors or cult of the dead which implies a continuity between past and present. At Corcomroe Abbey in County Clare I came across a young lad cleaning the headstones of the family graves. He told me he could remember the names of his people back as far as six or seven generations. In a niche lay the imposing effigy of Conor O'Brien who died in battle in 1267. The spot where he received his mortal wound had been remembered over the centuries, and is now marked for all time on a detailed map of the region. This is by no means an isolated example of Ireland's immense and insatiable communion with the dead which stretches back in an unbroken chain of being. Medieval, Celtic, Bronze Age, Neolithic and even Mesolithic ancestors still peer over the shoulders of the twentieth-century Irish; and their ghosts tug at the sleeves of the living.

What is it about Ireland that encourages such fanciful notions? Is there a dimension to reality here that is missing elsewhere? Were the Celts so very different from other European races as to have passed on a distinctive psyche? Of what were these proud warriors afraid, the Romans wanted to know: and the only answer they got from a captive Celtic chieftain was that the Celts were afraid the sky might one day fall upon their heads. It probably meant nothing to the Romans, but we can share that apprehension today since science has shown that the world could easily collapse around our ears.

The sites of Ireland's prehistory are better known than those of the historic period. This is only natural since the

The Giant's Gauseway, Co. Antrim, where legends have attached themselves to this spectacular formation of volcanic rock.

megalithic grave culture of the Boyne Valley ranks high among the great moments of human civilization of all ages and of all continents. Newgrange, that great 'house for the dead', was so much more than a tomb. Indeed, interment was just an element in a vast and complex existential metaphor which still challenges our intellectual ability as well as our creative imagination. Yet Newgrange was but the flagship of that culture, and there are many other megalithic sites in Ireland which, though less sophisticated, have conserved a greater dose of their environmental magic thanks to a remoter location beyond the reach of the tourist buses. The walk up the slopes of Slieve na Calliagh in County Meath leads to one of the richest experiences of prehistoric Ireland.

But who were the builders of these majestic structures? Archaeologists hate to conjecture, and we are told only that Ireland appears to have been part of a broad band of megalithic culture extending along the north-west seaboard of Europe and down to Brittany and Spain. More romantic souls look for an origin in the lost island continent of Atlantis, and see in Ireland the last outpost of that haunting civilization, for which no substantial proof exists, but which will not leave us in peace. If the memory of Atlantis is still inscribed, however faintly, in the Irish folk-psyche, then the Irish quest for America might be guided in part by that ancient longing to find a home beyond the rim of the western horizon. That this urge led to Atlantic City rather than Atlantis is one of those ironic quirks of destiny. The very fact that one comes across such hypothetical musing in the copious literature on Ireland must be a sign of something. An air of unresolved mystery hangs over the identity of the ancient Irish, and though that blood has since been diluted with that of all those who have since settled in Ireland, that certain Irishness of national character has prevailed.

But the story that unfolds in the pages of this book is not essentially concerned with such speculation. Instead, we embark on a series of journeys into the mists of the Irish past with our eyes on solid objects of ancient artefacts and architecture. These are the waymarkers or stepping-stones through the ages, fragmented remains of what was once a broad and well-maintained highway. Now there are many bits missing, and at places the chronological leap from one stone to the next is perilously long.

The Rock of Cashel, Co. Tipperary, where a royal seat of the ancient kings was transformed into a religious stronghold.

In prehistory we jump millennia from one paragraph to the next. At Mount Sandel in County Derry we encounter the traces of Ireland's first known inhabitants; but the scant vestiges of this 8,000-year-old seasonal camp-site are now hidden from view beneath a fresh layer of turf. Some might be disappointed to find nothing here, coming perhaps with a mental image of hearths still warm and smoking; but there is none the less a great pleasure to be derived from just standing on such a spot where prehistory was made. It is something intangible but real for all that: the historicity of place which sends a frisson up the spine.

A similar experience may be had at a beautiful sandy beach at Baginbun in County Wexford. There is nothing to hint at the importance of the place, but this was where in 1169 the landing occurred of the Anglo-Norman

Baginbun, Co. Wexford: site of one of the main landings of the Anglo-Norman invasions in 1169.

contingent of Raymond Legros, an incursion of feudal barons that was to have such far-reaching consequences for Ireland. A few bumps in the ground, now covered by tangled undergrowth, represent the bridgehead encampment. On the adjacent headland stands a Martello tower built some 200 years ago as a precautionary measure against an invasion by Napoleon. It is said, however, that lightning never strikes twice in the same place; and so far that has been true at Baginbun. This is a wonderful spot to experience history and to picture the boats of armed men discharging their supplies and equipment on to the unsullied strand. Now there is a sign asking visitors to leave nothing behind on the beach but their footprints. Just imagine the confused mass of footprints and hoof-marks as the band of Anglo-Normans scrambled up the cliff, hungry for the taking of Ireland.

This was the first wave of the campaign directed against the Celtic tribes of Ireland. For the conclusion of that process we go to another remote spot on the coast, this time in the far north of the country, at Lough Swilly in County Donegal. The year is 1607, and the defeated O'Neills of Ulster are taking ship into permanent exile in the poetically remembered 'Flight of the Earls'. Now Lough Swilly is mute and unforthcoming – for the surface of the water retains nothing of the passage of history. However, the place remains potent through our awareness that these were the last landscapes of Ireland that the great Earl of Tyrone, Hugh O'Neill, saw as the wind filled the sails of his craft and took it out to sea.

Very different feelings are evoked by the spot in Dublin's Phoenix Park where, on 2 May 1882, Lord Frederick Cavendish and T. H. Burke were the victims of a political assassination. Now all is peace and serenity beneath the neat rows of maturing chestnut trees. Elsewhere, a momentous turning-point of Irish history may be encapsulated in one compact physical object. The

Phoenix Park, Dublin: scene of an assassination in 1882 that was to have unfortunate consequences and claim more lives.

Treaty of Limerick of 1691, which concluded William of Orange's campaign in Ireland, is commemorated by the 'Treaty Stone' on which it was supposedly signed. This now sits, taciturn and glum, on a riverside plinth opposite Limerick Castle. Is this history reduced to a lithic lump? In vain may we contemplate the inert stone and expect enlightenment. Sometimes history can be felt as an absence rather than a presence. The lasting legacy of the

The Treaty Stone in Limerick is a reminder of broken promises and missed opportunities at a crucial moment in history.

Great Famine of the 1840s resides in empty hills and valleys, vanished settlements, dead and departed people. And in an environmental sense we can but yearn for the landscapes of the past, those rolling forests of oak felled for ships now sunk without trace and for houses long since burned out or rotted away.

These are important aspects of Ireland's past which add their own poignancy. But this book is mainly concerned with more substantial relics such as early monastic settlements, medieval castles and noble country houses. Here history presents itself in a more obvious way, providing us quite literally with a front door to step through and rooms to explore. We can make the intimate acquaintance of Cistercian monks, Franciscan friars, feudal magnates, city merchants and captains of industry through what remains of their buildings. Then there is the exquisite artistic legacy of the gold jewellery of the Bronze Age, the sculptural excellence of the high crosses and funerary chests. These latter are specifically Irish achievements which, though known, are deserving of wider appreciation and discovery by fresh generations.

Ireland's strongholds of stone express the constantly recurring theme of turmoil, strife, conquest and armed settlement. Some castles, such as Trim in County Meath, are aggressive statements, designed to impress, control and intimidate. At the other extreme, some are quite passive. The Bawn on a rocky islet in Lough Doon in County Donegal is as protective in intent as the shell of a barnacle; while Dun Aengus on the Aran island of Inishmore is as difficult of interpretation as it is fearsome to behold. Castle-building in Ireland continued as a serious activity well into the seventeenth century. The Scottish settlers of the 'Plantations' found that the baronial tower-house of their native land was ideally suited to their precarious position in a hostile countryside.

The idea of the castle returned in the nineteenth century to revolutionize the design of country houses which had enjoyed a century of Palladian and Neo-Classical elegance. At the beginning of the twentieth century a wave of revivalist fervour brought back into common usage a host of older ideas and motifs. The poet William Butler Yeats was very much at home in the Georgian salons of Dublin or the drawing-room of Lady Gregory's Coole Park in County Galway, but for his own

Thoor Ballylee, Co. Galway. This medieval tower was home to the poet William Butler Yeats from 1921 to 1929.

A rag tree at Dungiven Priory, Co. Derry, where strips of cloth represent the petitions of many supplicants..

abode he preferred the historic feel of a thick-walled medieval tower, Thoor Ballylee.

It was at Coole Park that Lady Gregory, patroness of the Celtic Revival, entertained the luminaries of the age. Like so many country houses in Ireland it is now no more than a mark on the ground, not a victim of the Troubles, but of that more deadly process of being overtaken by history and finding itself stranded in an alien age, a grandiose home lacking the means and the will necessary for its support. Yeats in his customary prophetic mood had foreseen in 1929 the demolition that ensued in 1941:

> Here, traveller, scholar, poet, take your stand
> When all those rooms and passages are gone,
> When nettles wave upon a shapeless mound
> And saplings root among the broken stone.

Coole Park is thus another one of those places eloquent by virtue of an absence of something. Even the ornamental lake has dried up. But there is one tangible souvenir of the people who once paraded here their wit and intelligence. A copper beech tree bears on its trunk the carved initials of some of Lady Gregory's house guests, most prominently the bold artistic flourish of the GBS monogram which presides over the more prosaic scratchings of the rest. Now an iron railing has been built round the tree to prevent lesser folk adding their own mark to the historic record.

At Fore in County Westmeath there is another tree which has suffered more grievously on account of its special status. This was a holy thorn of magical properties. Its wood could not be consumed by fire, so it was said. For this it became an object of veneration by pilgrims. At one point the custom began of hammering a coin into a fissure of the bark as a votive offering by the supplicants. Over the years the repetition of this practice has brought about the demise of the holy tree, of which only one atrophied segment remains, complete with mutilated coins wedged in the wood. Fore was also famous for a monastery built on a treacherous quagmire and water that ran uphill.

Pilgrimages to a profusion of such holy places in Ireland represent the most living link to the remote past. Rag trees at holy wells and processions to mountain tops such as Croagh Patrick in County Mayo take us straight back to the pre-Christian era of the Irish 'dreamtime' when the naming of the places by the ancient race brought to life the entire landscape in all its individual features. Celtic

Croagh Patrick, Co. Mayo. The hill where St Patrick once fasted is now the scene of an annual pilgrimage.

folklore recorded a history as well as a map of early Ireland; and though this has receded its memory is still cherished. The cult of Celtic legends crops up again and again in a variety of modern contexts. The 1920s family mausoleum at Mount Stewart House in County Down was endowed with the pre-Christian title of Tir Nan Og – Land of the Ever Young; and the memorial in the rebuilt General Post Office in Dublin to the Easter Rising of 1916 depicts the Celtic hero Cuchulain. It's not that people necessarily believe in the factual details of legends, but they do respect the intrinsic truth of the world of legend. After all, the bards have been silent for only 400 years, clearly not long enough to erase memories and feelings accumulated over a much longer period. It is hardly surprising that the names of the renowned places of ancient Ireland live on as potent symbols. Tara is more than ever a national emblem.

Ireland has been variously described as a time-capsule or a living museum, but these labels do no justice to that special Irish relationship to the past which is both instinctive and laced with a lively awareness of the present rather than obsessed with nostalgia. On the other hand, Ireland does generate a sizeable amount of retrospective self-analysis. At a modest farmhouse in County Kerry I spent a cosy evening by a peat fire in a room dominated by a massive glass-fronted Victorian bookcase. Most of the volumes it contained were on the subject of Irish history; and I thought it worth recording some passages from two of them.

Firstly, in an essay entitled 'The Romance of Irish History' by Roger Casement:

> The history of Ireland remains to be written, for the purpose of Irishmen remains yet to be achieved . . .
>
> Irish history is inseparably the history of the land, rather than of a race . . .

Tir Nan Og – the Land of the Ever Young – is the Celtic name given to a mausoleum at Mount Stewart, Co. Down.

Though pride of race is evident in the dominant Gaelic stock, their national sentiment centres not in the race, but altogether in the country, which is constantly personified and made the object of a sort of cult . . .

Wherever Irishmen have gone, in exile or in fight, they have carried this image of Ireland with them . . .

Ireland, too, owns an empire on which the sun never sets.

Then I came across a poem by John Hewitt, simply called 'Ireland':

We are not native here or anywhere.
We were the keltic [*sic*] wave that broke over Europe,
and ran up this bleak beach among these stones;
but when the tide ebbed were left stranded here
in crevices, and ledge-protected pools
that have grown salter [*sic*] with the drying up
of the great common flow that kept us sweet
with fresh cold draughts from deep down in the ocean.

So is Ireland a place or a state of mind? It's not the answer that matters, rather that the question is even put in the first place. And therein lies a characteristic of Ireland. People are concerned to dwell on such things, to look for their own essence and origins, and to conjecture on what might have been.

This book seeks to do no more than to probe and explore the significant places where that elusive Irish past breaks the surface of the present in a physical sense. The terrain surveyed is like a rich and intricate tapestry that is a patchwork of the efforts and endeavours of many successive ages. In Ireland today there is definitely a taste of history in the breeze – and a history that has in recent years moved out of the shadows and back into the wider European context that was enjoyed by this land of saints and scholars over a thousand years ago.

This carving of a medieval Irish bishop at Duleek Priory, Co. Meath, still retains its power and piety.

Poulnabrone Dolmen, Co. Clare. One of the most admired portal-tombs in the whole of Ireland is a landmark of the Burren.

HOUSES FOR THE DEAD

SIX MILES NORTH of Kilfenora and within sight of the modern road carving its way through the weird lunar landscape of the Burren in County Clare stands one of Ireland's best-known prehistoric monuments. The Poulnabrone Dolmen consists of a massive capstone of rough masonry resting on flagstones implanted in the ground. At regular intervals passing coaches stop, and tourists stare at the curious structure for a few moments before continuing their journey. More enterprising folk tread gingerly over the potentially ankle-breaking, fissured limestone pavement to get a closer look and take some pictures. The image of Poulnabrone has been recorded on celluloid times without number; its noble, sculptured outline has featured in many hundreds of books and brochures. To a certain extent it has become more than a symbol of the Burren: it has taken on a wider significance, expressing all the enigmas of Irish prehistory. Yet, the longer we look at it, the more abstract it appears; and the more physical facts we amass about it, the more its true meaning – whatever that may be – slips from our grasp.

Nevertheless, we endeavour to reduce it to comprehensible terms. First of all there is the obvious engineering problem, for which we can safely accept the mechanical explanation that the weighty capstone was hauled slowly and painfully up a temporary ramp, possibly with the aid of slender tree-trunks to act as rollers. Then there is the purpose of the enterprise; and the archaeologists are on hand to inform us that excavations have revealed the remains of twenty individuals, so that we can categorize it as a grave or tomb. Should we feel inclined to ask when it was built, then we are given various dates ranging as far back as the fourth millennium BC or more than five thousand years ago. And who built it? Neolithic (New Stone Age) peoples, we are told, who arrived in Ireland and other parts of Europe's Atlantic seaboard, originating we know not where, but reaching Ireland on a long migration via Spain and Brittany which also embraced Cornwall, Wales, Scotland, Orkney and Scandinavia.

There is thus an answer of sorts to most of the questions we normally pose about Poulnabrone and the other 160 dolmens or portal-tombs scattered about over the Irish landscape. Generally dated to the third millennium BC, the dolmens display a stunning variety of shapes and forms. But the type is instantly recognizable, whether it be the graceful, aerial elegance of the one at Legananny in County Down or the ponderous bulk of the mighty specimen at Browne's Hill in County Carlow, whose capstone of an estimated 100 tons is reputed to be the heaviest in Europe. Indeed, such was its weight that it was not possible to lift the colossal piece of masonry entirely clear of the ground, and one end has been left resting on terra firma. The dolmen at Kilfeaghan in County Down is by comparison a mere stripling of 35 tons, but it is none

Kilclooney Dolmen, Co. Donegal. This megalithic structure suggests a prehistoric essay in aerodynamics.

the less a vast dumpling of a boulder that appears to squat like an overweight toad. It was levered up somehow and underpinned by smaller stones.

What could be more beautiful than Kilclooney Dolmen in County Donegal? It has been likened to a bird poised for flight, even suggesting to one eminent archaeologist a prototype for the shape of Concorde. Like many of Ireland's prehistoric monuments it is set in a wild and lonely terrain. Geographical remoteness makes it easier for us to appreciate the full mystery of something that is also remote in time. However, not all of the ancient stones have escaped the groping tentacles of contemporary human settlement. Ballylumford Dolmen in County Antrim now finds itself marooned in a garden directly outside someone's front door, looking more like a folly than an ancient tomb. The impressive Proleek Dolmen in County Louth has sacrificed some of its original dignity to the local custom of tossing smaller pebbles so that they stay lodged on top of the 40-ton capstone. The legend has it that a wish is granted for every stone that stays put. If the procedure is at all efficacious then many folk have found satisfaction at Proleek; but the crowning heap of tiny stones detracts from the essential power of the structure. This is a pity, for as far as we can deduce the original intentions of the builders, it would seem that the dolmens were left largely exposed to proclaim the engineering triumph and to reveal the artistic effect of the naked structure.

The early Celtic inhabitants of Ireland, those master weavers of myth and legend, are mainly responsible for the popular names subsequently given to dolmens and handed down to us most commonly as Druids' Altar or Giant's Grave. A romantic tale has it that all the Irish dolmens were the beds of Diarmuid and Gráinne, that is, shelters erected each night during a year of flight from the wrath of Finn MacCool; for the intrepid Diarmuid had eloped with the betrothed wife of the elderly king.

The word 'dolmen' is actually derived from the Breton language, a separate branch of the Celtic family, meaning no more than 'stone table'; and the collective definition of 'megalith' to describe all prehistoric monuments of stone comes from two Greek words signifying quite simply 'big stone'. The concept of megalithic culture has thus been adopted as a convenient label to identify all those various groups of people who in prehistoric times are known to us for their prolific architecture of big stones. Ireland was one of their principal theatres of action in Europe, for the country fairly bristles with the remains of a frenzied building activity.

More numerous than the dolmens are the so-called

Proleek Dolmen, Co. Louth, is crowned with tiny pebbles as a result of a local superstition lost in the mists of time.

The wedge-tomb at Gleninsheen, Co. Clare, represents one of the main types of grave architecture in ancient Ireland.

court cairns: 329, or roughly twice as many, have so far been identified. They owe their name to their distinguishing feature of an open forecourt leading into a chamber covered by a mound or cairn. Their distribution is limited almost exclusively to the northernmost third of the country. The showcase specimen at Creevykeel in County Sligo is a sophisticated variant of the general type. It was once contained within a mound almost 230 feet long. Only the chamber was covered; and the forecourt, open to the skies, was paved with some form of slabs or cobbles. Just four cremation burials were found in the gallery in the course of the 1935 excavations, suggesting that the main purpose of the structure was related more to the space or court than to the needs of utilitarian interment. Thus the whole idea of the court cairn points beyond the strictly funerary to a wider ritualistic use, and it is not too far-fetched to see this category of monument as being akin to a miniature temple. Here for the time being reasonable conjecture must stop, but the nagging suspicion that the tombs may be more than simple houses for the dead cannot – as we shall see – be entirely banished from the mind, especially when we explore the most spectacular of the prehistoric 'cemeteries' at Carrowmore and Carrowkeel in County Sligo, and at Loughcrew and the Boyne Valley in County Meath.

But first we should take note of another category of grave known as the wedge-tomb, so called because the plan of the mound is noticeably wider at one end than at the other. The burial chamber within is typically long and narrow. One of the most sophisticated may be seen at Labbacallee in County Cork, whereas that at Gleninsheen in County Clare is of the simplest type, consisting of a box-like arrangement of stone slabs. An intriguing aspect of the wedge-tomb is the variety of interpretations read into it. On the one hand, it is considered to be 'the first all-Irish grave form' on account of the 387 known ex-

The court cairn at Creevykeel, Co. Sligo, is a complex grave of a sophisticated type which includes a small forecourt.

amples in the country. On the other hand, because it has similarities with tombs in Brittany, it is claimed as evidence that the builders of wedge-tombs were actually migrants from that region of France. As if in response to this apparent confusion there is now a shade of academic opinion which maintains that varying fashions in grave types do not necessarily indicate mass movements of people. Taking the analogy of Christian architecture in the Middle Ages, it can easily be appreciated that ideas can travel without vast migrations, invasions, or cultural suppressions.

Possibly more can be gained by looking at the similarities

Malin More Dolmen, Co. Donegal. This primitive dolmen appears pitched like a tent in the wild moorland.

rather than by totting up the differences. What we see from all the categories of megalithic tomb so far mentioned is that the Neolithic peoples of Ireland appear to have placed more importance on the afterlife than on the here and now of their existence. We have the remains of hundreds and hundreds of funerary-type structures built for eternity, whereas but scant traces have been found of domestic dwellings. These were made of wood, skins, thatch and wicker – the most ephemeral of materials; and there is no sign of any palaces or mansions of the ancient Irish. It is thus easy to form the impression of a widespread, collective otherworldliness, where the reality of the hereafter was what counted and the physical fact of human existence was but a transient illusion. The vision that surfaces in later Celtic legend of the magical realm of Tir Nan Og – the Land of the Ever Young – as the final stage of life may thus have its roots in the most distant mists of Irish dreamtime, a notion that was immortalized by those mysterious megaliths.

The apparent obsession for what we might still describe as houses for the dead reaches manic proportions at Carrowmore in County Sligo, Ireland's largest prehistoric 'cemetery'. At one time it was also the most extensive in Europe as well, but over the past hundred years more than two-thirds of the hundred or so megalithic tombs have been destroyed, mainly by gravel extraction. But what remains is still enough to form an idea of the original necropolis. The word is not out of place, for the landscape hereabouts was once peppered with funerary monuments to suggest a veritable city of the dead, perhaps a place where people came to die or were brought to be buried. To a certain extent this is confirmed by the discovery of actual human burials, but – as elsewhere – in quantities much smaller than the profusion of tombs would lead one to expect. Much of the mystique of Carrowmore has been diminished by the thriving agricultural activity of the area, but the great cairn known as Knocknarea – the legendary burial place of Maeve, Queen of Connacht – still holds itself aloof and majestic on the top of a nearby hill. The cairn is thought to contain a passage-grave, one of a type which constitutes the supreme achievement of prehistoric art and architecture in northern Europe.

Several fine examples of passage-graves are to be found at Loughcrew in County Meath in another of Ireland's magnificent megalithic 'cemeteries'. Slieve na Calliagh – or the Hill of the Witch – is the Irish name for the site and one which does more justice to the brooding remoteness of the terrain. An aerial photograph reveals that the monuments are scattered over several hilltops, with a

One of the grave monuments at Carrowmore, Co. Sligo, which make up Ireland's most extensive prehistoric cemetery.

concentration of passage-graves on two principal summits. Yet as you drive along the narrow road which runs between them you might easily miss seeing the great spectacle. Indeed, even as you climb up on foot through the sheep pasture, where ghost-like wisps of wool hang on the gorse bushes, to investigate more closely, there is no immediate indication of what awaits. The whole complex, dramatically sited though it is, cannot be appreciated until you have ascended the brow of one of the hills. Then you suddenly become aware of a huge central cairn adhering limpet-like to the summit and of a cluster of lesser tombs around it. The view over the lush Meath countryside is exhilarating, and with it comes the realization that the builders of the thirty or so grave monu-

The approach to cairn T on the summit of Slieve na Calliagh – The Hill of the Witch – in Co. Meath.

Slieve na Calliagh, Co. Meath – a glimpse inside cairn T is like an excursion into the Neolithic folk psyche.

ments had to heave, drag, or otherwise transport the stones to this lofty vantage point, no casual undertaking by any reckoning.

The prosaically designated cairn T is the largest on the eastern summit; and it provides a first intriguing glimpse of one of the earliest artistic ventures of Ireland's mega-lithic tomb-builders. The orthostat – or standing stone – to the left of the entrance is decorated with a variety of whorls and spirals, laboriously picked out of the surface of the rock. Enter the tomb – and you will need to have obtained the key from the local custodian – and penetrate the passage leading to a chamber with side recesses. Here the stones display a stunning variety of carved design: there are all manner of shapes from meandering lines, circles and diamonds to more accomplished radial patterns like a child's portrayal of a flower or the rays of the sun. The symbols – for that is what they appear to be – have been carved in a generous confusion without any evident regard for the overall composition. To our modern eye they may suggest experiments, exercises, or just doodling, but there is no way of telling for sure what significance it all had for the creators themselves. Standing inside cairn T on the Hill of the Witch is thus a weird experience. It's like being inside the creative, imaginative part of the prehistoric mind and enjoying a privileged, intimate view of its precious symbols and abstractions; but there are no explanatory captions, nor a key to aid in deciphering them.

In any case, perhaps we are wrong to be searching for precise meanings and tidy conclusions. After all, abstractions are meant to be just what they proclaim to be: abstract. Neither can any experts come to our assistance in this matter, though a psychologist of the Jungian school would be quick to point out that certain shared images, pictures, or archetypes inevitably float to the surface of the collective unconscious or folk-memory. Deprive us of all knowledge of our contemporary civilization and it would not be long before we started responding to natural phenomena such as the sun, the moon, water and lightning – echoes of which are here to confront us over a gulf of about five thousand years within the bowels of cairn T.

Any lingering doubts about the capacity of the Irish Neolithic to transcend the creative limits and to leap the barrier from tentative sketching to premeditated composition are instantly dispelled at the first sight of Newgrange, justly the most celebrated monument of its period in northern Europe. This is a triumphant coming together of all the latent spiritual, technical and emotional aspira-

tions of the megalithic culture, the crowning glory of a truly remarkable cluster of tombs in the Boyne Valley of County Meath. The satellite passage-graves of Knowth and Dowth in the immediate vicinity are also of the utmost importance in archaeological terms, but the accomplishment of Newgrange is more than enough to occupy the mind and to raise questions which apply quite generally as well as several with a unique relevance.

The initial impact of Newgrange, recently rebuilt after the excavations of 1962–75 and smartly clad in what was its original revetment of dazzling white quartz, is rather too modern for some tastes, but it does help tremendously to experience such a structure as well presented and in as good working order as it was when first constructed over five thousand years ago. The recessed entrance is deliberately adapted to ease the pressures of visitor flow – a brave but painful decision of the archaeologists – but the essential morphology is intact. The huge cairn is neatly contained within a girdle of decorated kerbstones which represent the maturing of the same artistic impulse witnessed at Slieve na Calliagh.

We are immediately confronted by an imposing recumbent entrance stone carved with a wild but confident array of spirals, including a striking triple spiral. This is no haphazard doodling but one of the great works of European prehistoric art. We may understand the swirling designs how we will. They have been interpreted as everything from a local map of the Boyne Valley's main tombs to an image of the universe, as symbols of underground water or a diagrammatic abstraction of the afterlife, or even as the sign of the Celtic triple goddess Brigid. Be that as it may, the power of the composition is overwhelming, with its mystifying triple spiral which suggests a seamless vortex of life force, without beginning or end, which is far beyond anything that our present binary perception of reality can properly comprehend.

Newgrange, Co. Meath; the reconstructed entrance to the most sophisticated and challenging passage-grave in Ireland.

Anyone who is troubled by notions that go beyond logical analysis might be better advised at this point to turn back and not enter the passage behind the entrance stone, for the implications of the internal secrets of Newgrange are truly astounding. The narrow passage extends up a slight incline 60 feet into the heart of the mound before reaching its final destination, a roughly cruciform chamber showing no great concern for symmetry. Look closely and you will discover a host of carvings of various motifs and of differing levels of competence. Many are on the backs of stones – including another splendid triple spiral – and are not immediately apparent. A corbelled roof, rising to a height of 20 feet, imparts a surprisingly lofty feeling within the tight confines of the tomb. Without doubt, this was in the pre-Christian period the most sacred spot in Ireland, so special that it became the focus of the much later legends of the Celtic centuries and remained inviolate until it was explored and excavated in modern times. Dating of the mound to 3200 BC increased its significance as a product of the native imagination and not the work of some foreign culture, thereby vindicating George Petrie's prescient plea over a century ago that we should 'allow the ancient Irish the honour of erecting a work of such vast labour and grandeur'.

All this would be impressive enough without the final touch which makes Newgrange such a special and endlessly intriguing phenomenon. Imagine the scene on 21 December 1967 when a group of archaeologists entered the tomb shortly before dawn to put to the test stories they had heard about the rising sun on the winter solstice penetrating the very core of the tomb. At 8.58 a.m. the first slender rays of sunlight shone through the opening over the entrance known as the roofbox, although a more appropriate description would be a megalithic fanlight. As the pencil of light widened to a beam and reached the central chamber, the cavernous interior was – according to notes made at the time – 'dramatically illuminated and various details of the side and end recesses could be clearly seen in the light reflected from the floor'. Then the light narrowed and receded back down the passage until it could be seen no more. The whole spectacle had lasted just seventeen minutes.

This deliberate alignment of the passage-grave to catch the rising sun of the winter solstice combined with the fact that very little burial material was actually discovered has led the archaeologists to question whether the primary purpose of Newgrange was really a tomb in the strict sense of the word; rather perhaps a structure of much wider implications, in which burial was just one of several elements, albeit the most important. In the earliest Celtic myths Newgrange figures as an abode of various gods and supernatural beings; and it was referred to in Irish as Uaimh na Gréine, or the Cave of the Sun. In both cases its sepulchral function is not mentioned, although it was later claimed as the ancestral burial place of the kings of Tara.

In recent years the enigma of the solar orientation of Newgrange has come to exercise imaginations not inhibited by the cautious approach of scientific archaeology. It has been pointed out that the mystery can be explained by the obvious practical benefit to a farming community of a device to mark the turning-point of the long, dark winter, a symbolic moment when the whole cycle of planting and harvesting may be perceived to recommence, offering an occasion of intense ritualistic significance. However, we are still faced with the need to find a bigger explanation to match the scale and sophistication of the achievement. It must have required a tremendous communal effort over many years to build the monument; and in any case Newgrange is no mere device and obviously means so much more than the sum of its parts. It can be seen as a vast and complex metaphor. But if so, then what does it stand for?

In this guessing game we are all free to let our imaginations take over where the known facts leave off. It has been suggested quite plausibly that the passage-graves in general are essentially fertility symbols rather than mortuaries. The argument proposes that their form represents a womb contained within a round megalithic belly. At Newgrange the simile can easily be extended to take into account the alignment of the passage as well. If the chamber is a symbolic womb then the rays of sun that reach it at the dawning of the winter solstice imply penetration by a solar shaft and consequently fertilization by the sun itself. Then the idea made manifest in the structure as a whole would be tantamount to an act of cosmic sexual intercourse, not necessarily a glorification of the act in itself but of the process of life's renewal or rebirth as expressed through a megalithic image of human reproduction.

But what role would the burials play in all this? If the cremated bodies, as has been suggested, were those of special people, a tiny élite, then the whole magnificent endeavour of Newgrange was thus a launching pad into eternity for a privileged few. But if these were token burials – albeit of special people – then their rebirth in the stone womb through the rays of the sun could have ensured the immortality of the community at large. Or was the desired fertility that of the soil, a matter of the utmost importance for the farmers of the Neolithic?

There is every reason to suppose that Newgrange embraced all that and much more. This powerful blend of death rites, cosmic and sexual imagery, and aspirations to an afterlife was the product of a culture which saw life and death as equivalent elements in a continuum of being, where the dead were still living on and the living were just those who were about to die. Yet there is nothing

Newgrange, Co. Meath. The mysterious triple spiral motif invites endless speculation. (Irish Tourist Board)

morbid about Newgrange. Its message is a celebration: its swirling spirals suggest a totality of existence encompassing both life and death. But inside the womb of New-grange there are no eggs awaiting fertilization, just ashes in basins of stone. Death leading to rebirth. What other conclusion can reasonably be drawn?

The potential meanings of Newgrange are quite simply overpowering. Superhuman in concept as well as execution, a most spiritual piece of architecture and engineering, it was the creation of a group of prehistoric Irish farmers who expressed in this way their passage through life. It was a direct product of their emotions, their guts and fibre, perhaps not a bid to achieve salvation but to commemorate the process in which they saw themselves inextricably bound up. Who can tell?

The construction of Newgrange must have been a cultural imperative and an ultimate statement of sorts. Once accomplished, there was no need for duplication: it stands at the zenith of prehistoric civilization in Ireland and nothing follows from it. In fact, the archaeological record goes rather quiet after Newgrange, almost as if the people who built it passed on gently into the Land of the Ever Young and pulled up the ladder behind them.

Within a few centuries part of the great cairn slipped,

The kerbstone of another imposing burial mound – at Dowth, Co. Meath – lies in the verdant pastures of the Boyne Valley.

Newgrange, Co. Meath. The powerful spirals on the entrance stone are a compelling masterpiece of Neolithic carving.

possibly as the result of an earth movement. Now it has been restored and is held in place by a concrete wall expertly hidden behind the revetment of white quartz. Blue-tits nest merrily enough in the crevices, introducing their own version of the reproduction process to the great monument. But the ghosts of the builders are as elusive as ever. We are left with more questions than answers. Yet even if the enigma of Newgrange will never be solved, this supreme accomplishment serves to remind us that some of the people of the New Stone Age possessed a knowledge and an awareness that have passed quite beyond our ken.

At Beaghmore, Co. Tyrone, the stone alignments and circles cover the landscape with their enigmatic patterns.

THE RIDDLE OF THE STONES

NOT ALL ENERGY in prehistoric Ireland was focused on the construction of graves: the passion for building with stones of great size extended – especially during the Bronze Age – to a whole series of circles and alignments even more puzzling than the monuments of the Neolithic. One of the most impressive examples of these new phenomena is to be found at Beaghmore in the Sperrin Mountains of County Tyrone. This vast complex was totally unknown until peat-cutting in the area began to reveal a grand and mysterious composition of standing stones. The first excavation commenced in 1945, and so far a vast ritualistic setting of well over an acre has been uncovered. To get an overall impression of the site it would be useful to be able to hover overhead and in this way to appreciate fully the geometric interplay of the seven stone circles and eight alignments which are associated with a dozen cairns. Not surprisingly, it has been suggested that the symbolism of Beaghmore was intended to be read from the sky by extraterrestrial beings.

It is evident that our imaginations are taken to full stretch to make sense of such phenomena. Some observers remark that the shape of the circle is basically a reflection of the orb of the sun, which was the principal element of pagan religious awareness. The circle in County Wicklow, known in English as the Piper's Stones, also bears the more ancient Irish name Buaile Acadh Gréine, or Enclosure of the Plain of the Sun. This might be seen as a lingering memory of what was the original significance of the circle, namely its relationship to the sun.

Most of the serious theories woven around stone circles in Ireland as elsewhere involve much speculation that the orientation of the settings was deliberately calculated to mark, observe, or record significant moments of the solar and lunar calendars. Astro-archaeology, as the discipline is sometimes known, claims much greater accuracy than conventional archaeologists are prepared to admit. At the extreme, the argument has become trivialized with one side asserting that the prehistoric peoples had built remarkably efficient and finely calibrated observatories, and the other side denying any such intent or achievement. The results of impartial research tend to suggest that there is in many cases a significant if not always accurate orientation towards events such as sunsets and sunrises at the winter and summer solstices. However, such knowledge would have been absorbed quite naturally by a society of farmers who spent most of their lives out of doors, and with little to distract them from observing the minutest details of the world about and above them.

In any case, when approaching the mute stones of prehistory it is always well to remember that the people who built or arranged them were human beings of flesh and blood, guided by down-to-earth as well as by high-flown ideas. Taking a more practical line, we may also view the stone circles and alignments as an early exercise in community architecture. The circles, in particular, are ideally suited for gatherings of groups on special occasions. There is in fact nothing at all mysterious about the form of the circle. It is the most natural thing in the world, as any group of tribesmen or boy scouts around a camp-fire instinctively know. Given the availability of suitable stones conveniently scattered about, it would be a challenge to human intelligence to use them to impose some sort of order and meaning on what was a wild and as yet formless landscape.

There may have been an even more practical imperative. If the land was needed for farming then any large stones on the surface over a wide area would need to be cleared and put somewhere. So in a sense the basic building blocks presented themselves, asking to be disposed of somehow or other; and the people brought an instinctive intelligence to the task and ended up by creating something that surprised even themselves. One of the stone circles at Beaghmore is remarkable for being filled with an enormous number of smallish stones (884 to be precise, for someone has counted them!), the sort of material that would normally have been heaped over a grave in the form of a cairn. One can only imagine that the stones were disposed of in this way because they were there in the first place. But once the work was done, the circle filled with stones doubtless acquired some special significance, if only because it was different. One has only to watch children at play to appreciate how an apparently casual act can quickly acquire a sophisticated meaning after the event. Interpretation of ancient structures is both an art and a science, as may be seen from the various theories advanced to fit the existence of the many solitary standing stones in Ireland. These range from the marking of ley-lines and burial places, ceremonial sites and tribal boundaries, to scratching posts for cattle. If the last-named function were to be correct, then the 23-feet-high specimen at Punchestown in County Kildare was tall enough to satisfy an elephant.

However, Irish stone circles and alignments – albeit with some exceptions – are generally composed of stones of modest dimensions by comparison with the great monoliths of Orkney, the Hebrides and Wessex. A distinguished architectural historian wrote of the circle at Drombeg, County Cork, that 'few of its stones are higher than a bar counter, and most of them about the height of a bar-stool'. In fact, part of the mystical charm of the two hundred or so Irish stone settings resides in their very smallness or intimacy of scale. We do not have to imagine a huge engineering operation conducted by a hierarchical society. It suffices to picture the circles being built by simple farming communities with no great pretensions, no planning committees or scientific experts, although there may have been itinerant advisers on stone circles just as there were masons travelling about in the Middle Ages. But the muscle power surely came from the local people, who were able for considerable periods to divert their energies away from their primary business of food production. In a sense all megaliths were the products of a society that had time on its hands.

The sites chosen for the circles must have been decided on only after very careful consideration, for the stones invariably appear to occupy a natural stage, to form a focal point for a vast panorama, and to offer an exciting arena to enter as well as an enticing prospect when viewed from afar. Let us see them then also as art in the landscape, but art in the widest possible sense to embrace the whole sphere of cultural knowledge and aspirations. What rituals were ever practised at such sites, we may only guess at.

The stone circle at Drombeg, Co. Cork, is on an intimate scale but it commands a majestic natural panorama.

Burials are frequent but by no means a hallmark of the genre. It is quite conceivable that the satisfaction of building the circles and alignments surpassed any other expectations. After that, perhaps just being there was their most important function. Are we making too complex a conundrum from the riddle of the stones?

The reconstruction of Mesolithic huts at the Ulster History Park shows the nomadic lifestyle of the hunter-gatherers.

PREHISTORIC LIFESTYLE AND ORIGINS

IT IS CURIOUS to write of Ireland, a country that has clung more doggedly than most to its ancient roots, that the arrival of the human species on its shores was, by European standards, relatively recent. Recent, that is, if you consider 9,000 years ago to fit that description. But we cannot be too dogmatic about this, for some traces of Old Stone Age settlement may yet be found. On the other hand, it could be that all vestiges of previous occupation were scoured away by one of the last glacial movements before the ice at last melted and released the land for colonization by flora and fauna alike.

According to conventional wisdom, Ireland's first identifiable human inhabitants came straggling over in small groups from south-west Scotland, and without getting their feet wet. For this spasmodic migration occurred during the last centuries before rising sea-levels gave Ireland its island status 8,500 years ago. The existence of an Argyll/Ulster causeway is borne out by the amount of relevant archaeological finds in the north-east corner of the country and their relative paucity elsewhere. Discoveries further south now indicate that there were probably several land bridges, principally via North Wales and the Isle of Man. It was thus by a variety of routes over dry land that Ireland's most ancient bloodstock may have found its way to a permanent home in the country.

By the very nature of their lifestyle as nomadic hunter-gatherers these Mesolithic (Middle Stone Age) people passed very lightly over the surface of the land. Theirs was an endless round of temporary camp-sites and provisional shelters constructed from pliant saplings tied together to form a tent-like framework which was then covered by animal skins and sods of turf. No ventilation other than by the single entrance was provided, and it must have been snug but smelly inside. Given the flimsiness of such dwellings, looking for traces of the Mesolithic is almost like hunting for prehistoric footprints in a landscape that has been changed beyond recognition. Occasional piles of discarded shells heaped up in middens close to the shore indicate the remains of countless Mesolithic dinners, but it is usually the presence of small flint implements, known as microliths, which provides the essential clue.

Among the thousands of pieces of worked flint discovered at Mount Sandel in County Derry were many microliths, mainly arrowheads and barbed devices suitable for hunting and fishing. More exciting was the revelation of a series of post-holes, pits and hearths, from which it has been possible to reconstruct the circular, wigwam-like shelters which are now to be found in Ireland's folk-parks. Examination of the food remains – an unglamorous but scientifically rewarding task – showed a variety of seasonal produce to suggest that the site was

Neolithic housing in Ireland was real architecture, as may be seen from this modern replica at the Ulster History Park.

occupied in summer as well as for much of the winter.

There must have been many other such places, regular camp-sites to which the Mesolithic groups returned time and again in the course of their peregrinations, but Mount Sandel, about a mile and a quarter upstream of Coleraine on a high bluff overlooking the Bann Valley, has given its name to that entire chapter of Irish prehistory. At the time of writing, however, the site itself appears to be seeking a degree of anonymity. Without signposts or any marking, it can only be deduced from the slightly different shade of green of an unprepossessing rectangle of grass wedged in between some woodland, an Anglo-Norman earthwork and a 1970s housing development. Nevertheless, there is a definite pleasure to be derived from a visit to the actual site of Ireland's earliest known human settlement, to experience that thrill when an abstract name becomes a physical reality. One could say that the story of the Irish people begins here.

It was during the lifetime of the Mount Sandel folk that rising sea-waters finally turned Ireland into the island it has remained ever since. The rupturing of the land bridges occurred around 6500 BC; and for better or for worse the Mesolithic settlers were here to stay. Not that they would have felt inclined to retrace their steps back to whence they had come, for their new home offered them a pleasant environment and an abundance of edible fish, game and plants. Viewed conversely, the severance of the links to Britain and between Britain and the Continent meant that those already established in Ireland at this time had the place to themselves for many centuries, perhaps even a millennium, before any fresh waves of immigrants with the necessary seafaring skills finally summoned up the courage to make the crossing by boat. The lack of a fresh infusion of blood probably resulted in a stagnating level of population, breeding from a fairly restricted genetic pool.

Farming settlements such as this at the Irish National Heritage Park were numerous during the New Stone Age.

All that was set to change by the beginning of the fourth millennium BC, if not earlier, when a fresh civilization and culture made its first appearance in Ireland. In terms of tools the Neolithic or New Stone Age had only a very narrow technological edge over its Mesolithic predecessor – an improved stone axe – but its people were bursting with new ideas. We always think of Neolithic folk in terms of stone – as the name indeed invites us to – for stone axes and megaliths were the most enduring material products of their civilization, and to us of the laser beam and microchip that has a primitive ring to it. But 'primitive' hardly matches the reality of these better-organized groups of highly resourceful people advancing remorselessly by land and by sea, possessing the knowledge and the skills to build houses, sail boats, clear forests, sow crops, practise animal husbandry, make pottery and even develop international trade. The trade in question was in axe-heads, for it was soon discovered that the highly valued rock known as porcellanite was readily available at two Irish sites, at Tievebulliagh in County Antrim and on the island of Rathlin. The products of these Irish 'axe factories' have been found as far afield as the Hebrides, north-east Scotland and southern England.

There is no reason to view the Neolithic take-over of Ireland as an organized military invasion of the Roman or Norman kind. The most probable scenario is of individual

Lough Gur, Co. Limerick – site of one of the most extensive prehistoric settlements – retains its archaic mystery.

The crannóg at Fair Head, Co. Antrim, is an excellently preserved specimen of an artificial island that was once inhabited.

groups responding to the pressures of an expanding population elsewhere, rather like the early European settlers in America who headed west in their convoys looking for pastures fresh. There were no covered wagons in this instance, but in other respects Ireland might have been at this time something resembling a New World. The Neolithic colonization of the country must have provided a saga or epic undertaking to rival that of the taming of the Wild West. It was surely a heroic enterprise, the launching of tiny craft on treacherous waters, carrying as well as people precious seedcorn and livestock, the latter trussed up for the voyage to prevent a fatal rocking of the boat.

There is no evidence of skirmishes with the Mesolithic

natives. Conceivably, there was room for everyone in the early stages and a gradual process of integration was possible. The skills and local knowledge of the hunter-gatherers would have been of great benefit to the efforts of the agriculturalists. The settlements were now permanent, year-round affairs, houses with wooden frames and walls of wicker or split planks. Several typical Neolithic houses have been reconstructed in recent years, based on information gained from the rectangular and circular foundations of the period discovered at Lough Gur in County Limerick.

Although only scant traces of some of the houses remain to be seen on the ground at Lough Gur, the place exudes a special enchantment. The lough, forming the shape of a horseshoe around a hilly promontory called Knockadoon, was an inviting spot for settlement: there was plenty of fresh water for drinking, cooking, washing and fishing, and good farming land close by sheltered behind low hills. The attractions of the site appealed to many generations of settlers and it became the focus of an extensive complex which comprised megalithic tombs, stone circles and ancient fields reaching down the millennia into the Bronze Age.

It is to the Bronze Age that the most distant origins of a typically Irish form of prehistoric dwelling may be traced: the crannóg or lake-house. About 250 of these artificial islands have been discovered, dotted about in Ireland's many inland loughs. They were created by pile-driving tree-trunks into the muddy bottom of the lough to form a solid foundation which was then further heightened, like a swan's nest, by the addition of branches and brushwood, as well as mud, peat and stones. Security, rather than easy proximity to good fishing, is thought to be the guiding principle behind the crannóg, since access was invariably not by a fixed link to the shore but by boat or even by a causeway just beneath the surface of the water.

We can picture the crannóg, complete with a palisade fortification, as being occupied by individual family groups, not in glorious isolation, but fairly close to others. This highly distinctive, aquatic style of residence enjoyed a long life after the Bronze Age and is especially associated with the Iron Age and early Christian times. The same sites could be reoccupied time after time, even after inundation, as was revealed by excavation at Ballinderry in County Offaly. Today the presence of a previous crannóg often shows up as a circular, flat mound on land that has been drained. Few remain as obvious artificial islands in the lake, though the specimen at Fair Head in Lough na Cranagh, County Antrim is really spectacular. This is a de luxe model, complete with a stone revetment to prevent erosion of its base.

The present state of archaeological knowledge does not permit any firm conclusions as to the exact origins of the people who brought their Neolithic civilization so successfully to Ireland. Some authorities see the builders of the megalithic tombs as part of a broad migration along the fringes of Europe which ultimately had its beginnings in the Middle East where the knowledge of agriculture was first developed. But the very early date of some of the megalithic tombs and their distinctive style indicate the spread of an autonomous culture through Spain, France, England, Wales, Scotland and Ireland.

Into this huge and remote region of uncertainty the proponents of the Atlantean theory launch themselves. They assume a highly evolved civilization of the lost island-continent of Atlantis spreading eastwards and its people finally fleeing their home in the Atlantic in the wake of a terrible natural disaster. According to this scenario Ireland's magnificent Neolithic culture would rank as the last outpost of the undiluted Atlantean race. This romantic vision of Irish prehistory – cavalier and fearless of academic refutation – is like the hot breath of a

This reconstruction of a crannóg at Craggaunowen, Co. Clare, illustrates the domestic architecture of the Iron Age.

poet against the cold voice of scientific archaeology. It offers no conclusive proofs, but it does provide explanations bold enough to meet the reality of the distinctive Atlantic dimension of European prehistory, a vibrant culture-province stretching along the entire seaboard from Spain to Scandinavia and with its heartland in Ireland. Atlantean origins are also claimed for the Celtic peoples of the Iron Age, with whose direct descendants Ireland eventually entered the historic era.

The golden neck ornament found at Gleninsheen is a tour de force *of ancient craftsmanship.* (National Museum of Ireland)

IRISH EL DORADO

THE ARCHAEOLOGICAL records of the Bronze Age in Ireland – roughly one and a half millennia from *c.* 2000 BC to *c.* 500 BC – contain most of the stone circles and alignments which still adorn the countryside. Apart from these impressive relics there is little of architectural note to point to any great progress over the Neolithic era. Nevertheless the Bronze Age must have been one of the most resplendent in Irish prehistory – quite literally a Golden Age – if we are to go by the evidence of a fabulous collection of finds of ornamental gold of an outstanding degree of artistic elegance and sophisticated craftsmanship.

The items now in the care of the National Museum of Ireland in Dublin tell their own story: a gold earring from Castlerea in County Roscommon, a gold torc from Tara in County Meath, a gold bracelet of ribbed design from Derrinboy in County Offaly. No fewer than 146 gold objects were discovered in a hoard in 1854 by the hill-fort of Mooghaun North in County Clare in the course of construction work on a railway line. Incredibly, many of the items were melted down for their monetary value, though casts of the destroyed pieces were made as a record of sorts. Collars, bracelets and neckrings made up the bulk of the 'great Clare find', which has been dated to the eighth and seventh centuries BC.

From the same county came the magnificent Glen-insheen 'gorget' or piece of neck jewellery, a bold composition which would still merit any number of design awards for its six concentric rings of ropework alternating with plain bands, and the whole contained within an outer and an inner ring of fine beading. The two extremities of the horseshoe-shaped ornament are further adorned by two concave discs, each with a pointed boss at the centre and a circular frieze of eleven small circles, composed of finely engraved concentric rings. Both Nordic and Phoenician parallels have been detected in this masterful design, either of which would be quite probable since there is every likelihood that Irish gold jewellery was much prized throughout Europe. Indeed, the very existence of such a rich artistic achievement points unwaveringly to a mature and confident civilization, capable of receiving and adapting the best of the ideas then in circulation. This was not a sudden outburst of creativity but the culmination of a tradition of gold craftsmanship going back to the earlier centuries of the Bronze Age. A superb example of the first known Irish gold productions is the crescent-shaped neck ornament discovered at Ross, County Westmeath, described rather poetically as a 'lunula' or 'little moon'; another beautiful item is the 'sun-disc' from Tedavnet in County Monaghan. Irish goldsmiths were still active well into the Iron Age, as evidenced by the Broighter hoard.

Despite such tremendous native artistry in gold – and the raw material itself was a product of the Wicklow Hills – the era bears the name of that alloy of copper and tin: bronze. The combination of the two metals produced a highly effective cutting edge which gave an enormous advantage in battle to those possessed of the secret of making it. Can we imagine itinerant ore prospectors and metalsmiths following their calling along the Atlantic seaboard in search of both clients and mineral deposits? Good quantities of copper ore were available in Ireland; and it has been shown that the copper mine at Mount Gabriel in County Cork was worked during the Bronze Age. Whether any tin was discovered in Ireland is at best uncertain, although forceful arguments have been advanced for small quantities of Irish tin being available. As things stand, the evidence points to Cornwall as the obvious source of supply; and it is probable that the refined metal was exported to Ireland.

Whatever the origin of the tin used in Ireland, let us admire the stunning production of bronzework made possible by the new technology. A mighty shield discovered at Lough Gur is representative of the martial equipment available by around 700 BC. Other large-scale items were the huge buckets and cauldrons, no mere cooking pots but symbols of great ceremonial significance which became essential trappings of power and prestige for centuries to come. Then there were the majestic curved bronze horns which probably sounded a triumphal fanfare during copious banquets. Smaller pieces included flesh-hooks for the kitchen, spearpoints and daggers for warfare, and, above all, those brilliantly designed and decorated axe-heads which have survived in great numbers.

The discovery of many axe-heads evidently flung into bogs and rivers as votive offerings shows that this piece of soldierly equipment was more than a token of a warrior's personal value; probably it reflected rank and authority as well. The exaggerated splayed profile of the cutting edge, broadening out from a relatively narrow stem, combines aesthetic values with functional efficiency. The decoration of axe-heads became something of an Irish speciality to add to the attraction of a product that found a ready international market. The export trade to Britain and the Continent has been attested by relevant finds. If St Patrick had not later given the Irish the shamrock as a national emblem, then the axe-head would have done just as well as a statement of national identity.

The sophistication of the industry and an idea of how it operated through the travels of expert metalworkers were demonstrated by the discovery at Bishopsland in County Kildare of a hoard of bronze objects including the tools of the trade belonging to a bronzesmith. We can only guess at the unhappy circumstances which led this wandering craftsman to conceal his precious equipment. He might have felt himself threatened and had the time to bury his load before preparing to defend himself. Whatever the threat he faced, the bronzesmith was prevented from reclaiming his property, which remained hidden from around 1200 BC until rediscovered some three millennia later. It is one of the frustrations of archaeology that, whatever we may deduce in broad terms of culture and lifestyle, the personal human dramas remain anonymous as to their protagonists and obscure as to their outcome.

However, let us content ourselves with the certainty that Bronze Age Ireland was one of the great centres of civilization of that era, truly in the vanguard of an expanding European culture, a veritable El Dorado of the prehistoric world. This was confirmed by further dramatic discoveries of gold artefacts in the autumn of 1990 near Wexford. Of the social progress which accompanied the material advances all too little is known. There was a

An Irish bronze axe head was a symbol of martial valour as well as a sturdy weapon. (National Museum of Ireland)

transition from communal to individual burial which may indicate a fundamental change of religious awareness. It is quite possible that a new concept of individual salvation might be detected here. If so, we should look to the Bronze Age as a significant turning-point for more than just metal technology.

Drumena Cashel, Co. Down. Though reduced in height, this stone enclosure reflects the defensive mood of its builders.

RATHS, CASHELS, CAHERS AND DUNS

ANYONE EXPLORING the ancient places of Ireland will soon be noticing the frequency with which the 'rath' or 'ring-fort' crops up. During the late Iron Age there was a vogue for these simple circular enclosures consisting of a bank with a ditch outside, which has left its mark on the countryside to this day. Recent estimates put the total number still in existence at more than thirty thousand; they are mainly recognizable as overgrown circles, often easier to make out in aerial photographs rather than on the ground. It is thought that many more have disappeared in the course of time due to the pressures of development; but the fact that so many have survived may be put down to the conservatism and superstitious respect of the farmers who considered the raths to be the abodes of the supernatural little people. To disturb a 'fairy-ring' could bring unwelcome consequences.

The raths are perhaps unremarkable in their present state, with their wooden palisades long since rotted away and their once mighty banks of earth and stone eroded by the elements to mere ridges of grass where sheep and cattle graze. But as archaeological evidence of the way of life of the broad mass of the Irish population over more than a thousand years, they form an invaluable record. Their very number invites us to generalize. They are not haphazard occurrences but relics of the most popular type of settlement which endured from the Iron Age through early Christian times and well into the Middle Ages, in some isolated instances even beyond.

It is often pointed out that the term 'ring-fort' is a misnomer since these enclosures were not built to withstand any serious military siege. Furthermore, the existence of a well inside a rath is extremely rare, so that any resistance to an organized attack would have been rather short-lived. But the idea of a fort does reflect, however imprecisely, the defensive attitude of the rath-dwellers. The danger they anticipated was almost certainly that from cattle-raiders, for rustling must surely rank among the oldest professions; and the rustlers were almost certainly rath-dwellers themselves. The enclosure was thus intended to offer temporary shelter for the livestock during raids as well as against attacks by wild beasts at night. It also meant a measure of security for the farmer, his family and dependants, who lived in huts inside the rath, homes which differed little from those in use during the Neolithic and Bronze Age. Now that these structures have vanished from the face of the earth, we are left with only the outer shell of the rath.

One item of interest to have survived at some raths is an underground chamber or 'souterrain'. This consists essentially of a stone-built passage of a type that would

A ring-fort at Craggaunowen, Co. Clare, shelters behind its wooden palisade to keep intruders at bay.

have been familiar to the builders of the megalithic graves. Entrance to the souterrain was via a trapdoor inside one of the houses; and a hidden exit gave access outside the rath. The picture we gain is of a secret passage that might be of use for the rath-dwellers to make a hasty escape in times of trouble. Alternatively, it can be seen as a bolt-hole where the women, children and elderly took refuge. But the refuge would have been temporary indeed, since it must have been very simple to smoke out the occupants. The most likely explanation is that the souterrain provided a vital few moments' respite before help could be summoned from one of the raths in the vicinity and the intruders could then be driven off by concerted action. But for most of the time the souterrain would have served as an excellent larder or storage chamber.

The rath was thus in essence a fortified farmstead, each one being occupied by a single extended family and located not too far away from others of the same tribe. It was the most basic element in the pattern of the Irish countryside, the essential stitch in the rural fabric. Whereas England was making a patchy transition towards urban living under the Romans, and later to nucleated villages under the Saxons, the Irish retained the old ways of scattered settlements. Although the country is now well endowed with towns and cities, the rural areas are still noticeably under the influence of the tradition of scattered settlement. Today's isolated homesteads and smallholdings are the natural descendants of the now deserted raths.

When is a rath not a rath? When it's made of stone, it's usually called a cashel. One of the finest specimens of the genre is Drumena Cashel in County Down, and it comes complete with a souterrain. Slightly larger and more defensive than a cashel are the cahers and duns. Often referred to as stone ring-forts, these grander productions of drystone masonry really do warrant the designation.

Superbly built and with an acute sense of strategic location, these stone ring-forts – to be found principally in the rocky terrain of the west – are tremendously satisfying places to visit. The posture of defence may now be experienced as scenic charm at Staigue Fort in County Kerry which squats purposefully in the middle of a picturesque valley commanding a distant view of the sea. Its stance is watchful, its single entrance ever vigilant like the eye of a Cyclops, rather reminiscent of the brochs of Scotland. The much-restored Grianán of Aileach in County Donegal perches on a lofty hilltop, with a beady eye on Lough Swilly and Lough Foyle, enjoying an elevation that would have recommended itself to one of kingly ambitions; and indeed it was the royal seat of an O'Neill sept for several centuries. The dwellings within the fort have gone, but the stone bastion endures as a reminder of human mortality, a feeling so beautifully expressed in an old Irish poem inspired by Rathangan:

> The fort remains after each in his turn,
> And the kings asleep in the ground.

It has been suggested that stone ring-forts such as Staigue and Grianán of Aileach were built primarily for show, as a parade of wealth and status, and generally to impress. But their defensive potential should not be dismissed out of hand. Security rather than bravado was surely the moving force behind the construction of the remote and mysterious Bawn or Doon Fort on a rocky islet in Lough Doon in the depths of Donegal. This is one of the most magical and atmospheric of ancient sites in Ireland. For some reason it is not listed as a National Monument and does not figure in many guides; nor is it signposted. A narrow road takes you as far as a small cottage where for a modest sum an old-fashioned clinker-built rowing boat may be hired. Lough Doon itself is a short distance away along a footpath, and the boat is

The small entrance of Staigue Fort, Co. Kerry, commands a distant view along the valley to the sea.

The outside world, as viewed through the front door of The Bawn, an island stronghold in the waters of Lough Doon.

beached on a narrow strand. From here there is as yet no sign of the Bawn; and so you row out through a curtain of reeds into the dark, peat-coloured waters of Lough Doon.

Fairly soon the circular drystone wall of the ring-fort comes into view. At first it appears to emerge from the lough like a crannóg, but the Bawn is built on rock-solid terra firma. Outside the main entrance there is a grass-covered ledge. The interior is happily overgrown with weeds and nettles, out of which neatly curving stairways lead to the top of the wall which is intact for almost the entire circuit to a height of more than 10 feet. From this circular rampart there is a glorious prospect of some of the loveliest scenery in Donegal. A more appealing hide-out would be hard to imagine, for this is an absolutely perfect stronghold set in a natural moat. Its only weakness would be that the surrounding hills would cover the approach of would-be aggressors, who could lie in wait for the occupant of the Bawn to emerge like a crustacean from its shell. An ambush would then be relatively simple to arrange. It is thus reasonable to assume that the entire district was held by the chieftain in question and that the land all around his watery lair was occupied by people he could call his own.

While it is possible to work out some sort of plausible scenario for the Bawn, there is one mighty work of defence which defies any conclusive explanation. Dun Aengus on the main Aran island of Inishmore, perched on the very edge of 270-foot-high sheer cliffs, is not really a ring-fort in the conventional sense, for it consists of three semicircular concentric rings of drystone masonry. The diameter of the semicircle is in no need of fortification since it is formed by the cliff edge itself above the mighty Atlantic, whose swell slams into the solid rock far below in a remorseless series of body blows. In physical terms this is the most memorable and powerful of places. Visitors to this westerly outpost of Europe enter easily

The circular wall of The Bawn is in remarkably good repair, although first constructed many centuries ago.

into conversation with one another, the sense of companionship stemming perhaps from a shared feeling of insignificance and precariousness. At times you feel that a stiff wind could blow everyone off this exposed ledge of rock with no trouble at all.

Beyond the three walls of stone the defences of Dun Aengus on the landward side are further enhanced by a field of huge stone slabs stuck forcefully into the ground at menacing angles, quite enough to halt a regiment of modern tanks in their tracks. And herein lies the heart of

Dun Aengus – the menacing stone defences of the chevaux de frise *presented an awesome obstacle to any assailant.*

the enigma of Dun Aengus. Against what enemy and what equipment was this ancient Irish Maginot Line intended to serve? The occupants of the fort, with their backs to the open Atlantic, appear to have dug themselves into a last-ditch defensive position. The bristling stone stakes, for which the technical term is *chevaux de frise*, have been explained away casually by the theory that the slabs just happened to be conveniently available lying on the surface of the land and that it was just a matter of rearranging them. It is evident that such weighty material had to be ready to hand, but the labour involved in such an extensive formation was truly Herculean. The imperative to build such a defensive system must have been compelling and absolute.

Archaeologists generally assign all the stone ring-forts to the centuries immediately before and after the birth of Christ. If the dating is correct then we can perhaps see the Celtic tribes of Europe, displaced by the advance of Roman arms, as the incursors against whom the defences of Dun Aengus were erected. There is also the possibility that Dun Aengus might have been built by one of the Celtic tribes fleeing before the Romans. It could have been the Belgae who, with memories of massacres by the Romans fresh in their minds, fled into exile as far west as possible, before finally staking out their territory when they had reached the very rim of the known world. It is recorded by Tacitus that Agricola did give brief consideration to an invasion of Ireland, but other priorities intervened. Conceivably, the terrified Belgae on Inishmore were not minded to take any chances. The perceived threat which motivated the builders of Dun Aengus was clearly one of alarming proportions.

The Atlantologists have their own theory about Dun Aengus, which they place much earlier in time and interpret as a defence against aggressors not from the east, but from the west, namely the people of the lost world of Atlantis. According to this idea, the devastating cataclysm which sundered the Aran islands from the Irish mainland and drowned Atlantis for good also caused the rocky hill on which Dun Aengus sat to split; with the result that half of the fort collapsed into the sea. This fascinating idea is difficult to reconcile with the accepted

Dun Aengus – a pleasing abstract pattern emerges from the stonework of this obdurate stronghold on the Aran Islands.

chronology of the site, but it does serve to underline the fact that the mystery of Dun Aengus is far from being solved. In any case, a healthy dose of enigma adds to the exhilarating presence of this most magnificent of monuments, whose true significance is veiled by the mists of prehistory.

The Turoe Stone, Co. Galway, is a spectacular display of Celtic motifs and a most accomplished work of sculpture.

HIGH KINGS AND TALL STORIES

SET IN A FIELD in front of a neat farmhouse at Turoe in County Galway there stands a round stone, some 3 feet in height. Even a casual glance reveals that this is something quite different from the untooled, rough monoliths of the Bronze Age. For this compact granite boulder is covered with carvings of a most delicate and accomplished character. A swirling, curvilinear, abstract design has been miraculously conjured out of the obdurate rock by picking back the stone to leave the actual pattern standing proud in relief. The lively interplay of spirals, curves, circles, triskeles and trumpets has been convincingly identified as related to the La Tène period of Celtic culture in continental Europe. This would date the stone to around 300 BC. Not that the Turoe Stone should be seen as a European product deposited on Irish soil, for its weight alone would have caused major problems of transport; and it is most probable that it was carved here on the spot. Whatever its symbolic significance may have been – phallic, omphalic, or other – its artistic affinities with the wider world of the Celts indicate that Ireland during the Iron Age was already part of a European Celtic civilization. Thus the Turoe Stone and another of very similar type at Castlestrange in County Roscommon confront us not just as prehistoric works of art, but with proof incontrovertible that a distinctively new culture had made its dramatic appearance in Ireland.

The Celtic inheritance is the most emotive and at the same time most mysterious chapter in the story of the Irish nation. While it is generally believed that it is Celtic blood and genes which give the Irish their special character, outlook and artistic vision, there is absolutely no firm account as to the date of arrival of the Celts in Ireland, how they assimilated with the existing population and – most importantly – whence they came originally. According to some experts, the Celtic tribes of central Europe expanded rapidly during the early Iron Age, migrated to the north and west, spilled over into Britain, and so on into Ireland. Other accounts, including those contained in Irish legends, have the Celts arriving via Spain. And there is also the Atlantean theory that the Celts were the direct descendants of the people of Atlantis who had fled to the Mediterranean and Middle East several millennia earlier. If so, Ireland was the closest they could get to their lost home beneath the waves of the Atlantic. Be that as it may, it is now thought that the Celtic influx into Ireland goes back much further in time than previously supposed.

There is also some confusion as to the nature of the Celtic arrival. The theory of outright invasion by vast numbers in tribal groups has given way to that of a more peaceful, less spectacular process of infiltration and gradual assimilation. Whichever way it occurred, there is no doubting the combined emergence of the Irish language, the technology of iron, and a warrior aristocracy. This élite consisted of a profusion of chieftains ruling small tribes or kinship groups – the *tuatha* – scattered all over the Irish countryside. Their economy was based on farming and cattle-raising, with the latter activity finding a special place in the folklore of the period. For it is as cattle-raiders or rustlers that we often encounter the early Irish chieftains in the ancient myths and legends that have been recorded. We may surmise that this unruly activity was motivated by a potent blend of sport, adventure, prestige and natural human aggression coupled perhaps with the basic urge to survive – if need be – at the expense of one's neighbours.

It is not without significance that the fantastic deeds of the warriors of the Ulaid and of their great hero Cuchulain, as narrated in the ancient epic *The Cattle Raid of Cooley*, or *Táin Bó Cuailnge*, revolve around the attempts made by Queen Maeve of Connacht to steal the famous Brown Bull of Cooley belonging to the King of Ulster. It is surely reflective of the endless tussles over cattle that a major war between two tribal kingdoms is portrayed as a larger-than-life tale of rustling in high places. As the army of Queen Maeve approaches the border of Ulster, the scene is set for heroic actions that will need to surpass anything previously accomplished: for a mysterious sickness has incapacitated the entire host of Ulstermen except for the seventeen-year-old Cuchulain. The as yet unbearded youth takes up his position by a ford of the River Dee where he is able to take on the enemy one by one in single combat. Needless to say, Cuchulain slays all the men pitted against him, and even finds time amidst the swordplay to lay low more than a hundred of the foe

Celtic decoration adorns this sculptured stone at Castlestrange, Co. Roscommon; but its symbolism is unclear.

with his slingshot. In a memorable image to describe his amazing agility we are told that he could turn around so fast that his skin was left standing where it was facing. Eventually the Ulster army recovers from its sickness and comes to the rescue. The boy wonder Cuchulain has not even a scratch on his body. But joy is not unconfined, for the tale ends with the Brown Bull of Cooley going insane, bursting its heart and finally falling dead on its hooves.

The debilitating disease inflicted on the men of Ulster was a punishment, so runs the legend, for the death of a woman called Macha. Now Macha was somewhat of an athlete, and her husband boasted that she could even outrun the horses of the King of Ulster. In spite of being pregnant she was forced by the king to run against his chariot. Although she won the race, she gave birth prematurely to a boy and a girl and then died on the spot, but not before placing a curse on the warriors of Ulster that they should be rendered weak and powerless for nine days whenever threatened by an enemy.

Whether factual or mythical or something in between, Macha is much more than a tragic figure in a remote legend. Her existence is associated with an impressive mark on the landscape in the shape of a ritual hill just outside the city of Armagh. More commonly known today as Navan Fort, its original name was Emain Macha; and it served as the ancient capital of Ulster. However, it would be misleading to impose our modern idea of a capital city on a place such as this and to expect to find the ruins of a palace, administrative buildings and an urban apparatus. Just as ancient Irish kingdoms were fluid concepts rather than rigid nation states, so the capital was a ritual spot rather than a permanently occupied stronghold or citadel. We must imagine the kings as semi-nomadic or at any rate peripatetic as they travelled about their territory for much of the time in order to reinforce the loyalty of their bands of warriors, the *fianna*. The capital was thus a

symbolic place for inaugurations, rituals of kingship, assemblies, receiving submissions, holding court and consulting oracles. Here at Navan Fort, there is nothing – despite the name – to suggest that defence was a prime consideration. For the 18-acre circular enclosure has its ditch inside the bank, thereby handing a clear advantage to any assailant from without. Within, on the summit of a low hill, there is a flattish artificial mound which is not at all impressive in physical terms but which conceals the evidence of a remarkable prehistoric enterprise whose true motivation is unlikely ever to be fully understood.

Excavations carried out between 1963 and 1971 involved the lifting, examination and reconstruction of the mound. It was discovered that the site had been occupied in the late Bronze Age around 700 BC by a circular house set within a shallow enclosing ditch. A number of fine bronze items such as an axe, spear-heads and a sickle were unearthed. Continuity of occupation into the Iron Age was documented by a number of typical objects of the period, showing that the settlement bridged the two great metal eras. The circular houses in themselves are no sure sign of anything special, but the fact that they were continuously rebuilt over such a long span of time is taken as proof that the place was endowed with some significance. The exotic find of the skull of a Barbary ape raises the prospect that this animal was a gift from a king in Spain or even North Africa to someone of equivalent status at Navan Fort, quite possibly a king of Ulster.

All that is fascinating enough but the archaeologists discovered something of far greater import. From the remains they deduced that the round houses were demolished at a later stage, and in their stead one huge circular structure of gigantic proportions was erected. Five concentric rings of wooden posts were driven into the ground, presumably to support a massive, conical roof.

The lack of household debris points to a non-domestic, probably symbolic use of the building as a sort of temple or focal point of an extensive ritual landscape which included the magical waters of the nearby Lough na Shade. At the centre of the structure there stood a great post, much bigger than the others, which probably served as a totem. It was the remains of this central post which enabled scientists to put an accurate date of 100 BC to the building.

Very soon after completion, perhaps not even ten years, the great round house was systematically filled with an abundance of limestone boulders to create a mighty cairn. Once this was done the protruding posts and outer wall were set on fire, and finally the mound was covered over with earth and sods, leaving essentially what we see today. What an extraordinary sequence of events! If it had been an enemy attack then the aggressors would surely have spared themselves the trouble of transporting such quantities of stones inside the building before putting it to the flames of destruction. But if this was a ritualistic act by the people of Navan Fort themselves, then its potential religious significance escapes us. At any rate, the notion of converting a round 'temple' into a solid mound of stones and earth was an act conceived and carried out by people who were not afraid of bold, even revolutionary changes. This then was the real origin of the place which became enshrined in the epic poems of the Ulster Cycle as the mythical capital of King Conchobar (Conor) mac Nessa, home of Deirdre of the Sorrows and of the hero Cuchulain. Emain Macha or Navan Fort has been described most aptly as an Irish Camelot; and like its Arthurian counterpart it presents us with a curious blend of fact and fantasy, hard material evidence and evanescent figments of legendary tales, knotted strands which are now impossible to unravel.

The same tantalizing mystery is present at Tara, most potent and poetic of the early Irish royal sites. This became the most prestigious of all the ritual sites, the seat and inauguration place of the High Kings of Ireland. As at Navan there is nothing to point to the existence of any form of royal architecture. The so-called 'Banqueting Hall' is a rectangular shape on the ground, most probably Neolithic, which owes its name to a medieval literary reference. Just as Arthur's Camelot has endured as an anachronistic vision of the Middle Ages, so royal Tara continues to conjure up images of some sort of palace of medieval style which never existed. Rather it resembled an open tribal area of assembly set within a hilltop enclosure with the ditch located inside the bank, as at Navan Fort. Nor is the 'Mound of the Hostages' at Tara the work of the High Kings but a much earlier cairn built over a megalithic tomb. Tara thus presents us with much in the way of chronological confusion, but the important fact to retain is the intense sanctity of the spot which endured from the last centuries of the pagan era well into Christian times.

Whether the *Ard Ri* or High King of Ireland was a real power in the land or more the product of a fertile poetic imagination is difficult to assess. In all probability, any claimant to that elevated rank and title would have discovered that his writ did not extend everywhere. In fact, the general picture of the early Irish kings and chieftains is of constantly shifting alliances and of localized spheres of influence. The rivalry between Ulster and Connacht is already manifest in *The Cattle Raid of Cooley*; and between Navan Fort and Tara there lies in the south of County Armagh a mighty linear earthwork called the Dorsey, whose purpose can only be defensive and which hints at very real fears of neighbourly aggression and invasion.

A number of other royal capitals have been identified: Cruachan for Connacht, Dun Aillinne for Leinster and

Navan Fort, Co. Armagh – the scene of epic events recorded in the legends of the ancient kings of Ireland.

Cashel for Munster. These are all places which command extensive views. The ceremonial hilltop in County Westmeath known as Ushnagh enjoys a particularly wide panorama, claimed to encompass twenty of Ireland's thirty-two counties on a day of exceptional clarity. A stone in the shape of a cat is said to mark the spot where the five ancient provinces of Ireland converge. There are many other lesser mounds which were once the inauguration sites of local kings and chieftains, such as Magh Adhair in County Clare belonging to the Kings of Thomond. One of that line named Lorcan was challenged here to a game of chess by Flan, the High King of Ireland, in an intriguing variation on conventional battle tactics. The image of the two warriors crouched in concentration over a chessboard must have caused mirth as well as uncertainty among the rank-and-file of the rival armies.

But the magic of Tara remains supreme; and the real importance of the place in history is borne out by the discovery of a number of Roman artefacts which prove that the occupants of Tara were in correspondence at some level with a part of the Roman Empire. Tacitus informs us that Agricola 'saw that Ireland ... might prove a valuable acquisition', and that he boasted that the country could be taken by 'a single legion with a moderate band of auxiliaries'. But Agricola's claim was never put to the test; and so the Celtic world of the Irish Iron Age was able to survive for roughly a thousand years without a Roman interregnum. The non-arrival of the Romans in Ireland has been well described as 'a momentous non-event', for it allowed the country to pass culturally intact from the pagan Celtic into the Christian Celtic era without any Classical dulling of the edges.

The oral traditions of the Iron Age were handed down from generation to generation, gathering embellishment on the way, and were eventually committed to writing many centuries after their original formulation. One of those scribes who, in the twelfth century, diligently copied out *Táin Bó Cuailnge*, the chief saga of the Irish, added his own opinion: 'But I, who have written this history, or rather fable, am doubtful about many things in this history or fable. For some of them are the figments of demons, some of them poetic imaginings, some true, some not, some for the delight of fools.' However, it would be wrong to dismiss the early Irish legends out of

The Hill of Tara, Co. Meath, where myth and prehistory co-exist in a potent symbiosis of national significance.

A marvellous specimen of Ogham script consisting of notches cut on the edge of this monolith at Breastagh, Co. Mayo.

hand as tall stories; and it is wiser to approach them with the same sort of respect accorded to the Homerian epics, being mindful of their inner essence rather than their literal truth.

Even without fanciful embellishment, the historical facts and realities of Ireland in the early centuries of the first millennium AD are impressive enough. The Irish were strong and sufficiently confident to harry the Romans in their province of Britannia, and later to establish a sizeable Hibernian empire of their own from the beginning of the fifth century. The Irish colony of Dalriada expanded remorselessly at the expense of the Picts and completed the final conquest of the country which still bears the tribal name of the Irish Scoti: Scotland. The Irish colonization of parts of western Britain was recorded by the renowned Cormac of Cashel (d. 908): 'The power of the Irish over the Britons was great, and they had divided Britain between them into estates ... and the Irish lived as much east of the sea as they did in Ireland, and their dwellings and royal fortresses were made there.' It was clearly a time of buoyant expansionism and cultural supremacy for Ireland. Some of the leaders of Irish society at that auspicious moment are commemorated by those pillars of stone carved with the curious notches of the Ogham alphabet along their edges. The conversion to Christianity added a fresh lustre to the culture of Ireland. Native energy and creativity were to find a new outlet in the Christian faith; and the Irish went from strength to strength carrying the banner of their belief in Christ.

A bizarre collection of ancient sculpture bides its time in the chapter house of the Church of Ireland cathedral, Armagh.

FACES FROM THE DISTANT PAST

THE ART OF the Iron Age, abstract and impenetrable, affords us hardly a glimpse of the physical appearance of the people of Ireland. But there is in the city of Armagh a unique opportunity to see a bizarre collection of figurative sculpture. Ask to be admitted to the chapter house of the Church of Ireland cathedral, and you go through a discreet door in the north transept. At first there is nothing much to see, but then you might notice a jumble of ancient stones cowering in the corner like obscure objects of shame, as if their obvious pagan inspiration might yet be capable of some unhealthy magic.

There is a rampant figure wearing what could be a head-dress and a short skirt, looking more like an ethnic Indian product of South America than a Celt of Ireland. Next to it there stands a more passive figure, legs parted and arms hanging lankly, and with a swept-back hairstyle which has been likened to the rays of the sun. But the star of this motley crew is the so-called Tandaragee Idol. The sculpture is small – just about 2 feet tall – but its effect is powerful, even disturbing. The head is oversized and the lines of the face stand out strongly. The mouth is framed by the continuous circuit of a beard and moustache, but the cheeks are cleanshaven. The neck is massively thick, like that of a prize bull. The figure appears to be wearing a helmet of sorts, from which the stumpy remnants of what may have been horns protrude. The overall martial character and barbaric mien have been interpreted as evidence of the pagan identity of the statue; but it is not possible to judge whether this was an actual portrait in stone of a real person or an idealized general type.

Straddling the borderline between paganism and Christianity are a number of carvings in stone to be encountered in County Fermanagh. On Boa Island there is the eerie two-faced human representation known as a Janus figure. This is a strong and confident composition dominated by huge, staring eyes and an unnaturally pointed chin. The beard is a slightly more elegant version than that worn by the Tandaragee Idol. Not far away along the shores of Lower Lough Erne in the churchyard at Killadeas a slab of stone bearing two carvings is implanted in the soil: the earlier is a crude but almost expressionistic portrayal of a human head in full relief on the edge, and on the flat face of the stone there is a delicately executed image in half-relief of a cleric striding out with staff and bell. Known as the Bishop's Stone, this single slab might well document the transition from paganism to Christianity in its two subjects, but not enough can be deduced about the identity of the face on the edge.

The famous 'Tandaragee Idol' portrays a warrior who would have proved to be a formidable adversary.

Whichever side you view, this double-faced Janus figure on Boa Island, Co. Fermanagh, offers few clues to its identity.

White Island on Lough Erne, Co. Fermanagh contains the most moving collection of early Christian sculpture.

Just a short boat-ride away lies White Island, just one of many hundreds scattered about in the waters of Lough Erne, but this island is famous on account of the eight magnificent statues discovered there and which have been mounted in such a dramatic fashion on the wall of a ruined monastic church. Here we have both feet planted firmly on Christian soil, for we are reliably informed that the figures represent clerics; but there is an otherworldly dimension to the faces. The expressions are suggestive of some form of meditation, either bearing the faintest wisp of a smile or open-mouthed as if still breathing. It is all quite mysterious and compelling.

St Patrick's Well at Clonmel, Co. Tipperary, offers a potent blend of sanctity, antiquity and tranquillity.

FOR ALL THE SAINTS

THE HILL OF SLANE in County Meath is noted for the ruins of a sixteenth-century Franciscan friary but the real significance of this picturesque spot overlooking lush farming country is as the site of one of the most dramatic incidents in the conversion of Ireland to Christianity. The story goes that St Patrick ascended the Hill of Slane and camped on the summit where he lit the Paschal bonfire in the year 433, marking Ireland's first celebration of Easter. Both the time and the place of this simple act had been carefully chosen in order to deliver a symbolic challenge to the pagan High King Laoire at nearby Tara. For Easter clashed with an important pagan festival and it was the prerogative of the High King on this occasion to light his fire before all others. Furthermore, the Hill of Slane and Tara were within easy visual contact with one another. Not content with this very public act of defiance, St Patrick then made his way to Tara where, in the presence of Laoire, he won a victory over the druids in a contest of magic. Laoire's reaction to St Patrick was statesman-like in the extreme: although he declined conversion for himself, he allowed those of his people who wished to embrace Christianity to do so.

Another astute and premeditated act was perhaps St Patrick's choice of the 2510-foot high mountain in County Mayo which is now known as Croagh Patrick, for his withdrawal from the world for the forty days and forty nights of Lent. Perhaps the peak was already venerated as a source of earth magic, but in any case Patrick demonstrated to all the kings and chieftains of Ireland that he could rise even higher than their royal mounds. It was reputedly during his sojourn on the scree-strewn slopes of Croagh Patrick that the saint summoned to his presence a great host of loathsome and venomous creatures, which he then commanded to cast themselves over the edge of the mountain. By popular tradition, the proof of this Christian magic is supplied by the absence of snakes in Ireland to this day. It was a fact known to the eighth-century scholar the Venerable Bede, who wrote confidently about Ireland: 'No reptiles are found there; for though often carried thither out of Britain, as soon as the ship comes near the shore and the scent of the air reaches them, they die.' The truth of the matter is more prosaic: the severance of the land bridges between Ireland and Britain occurred before snakes and some other reptiles and animals were able to extend their territory that far.

The legends surrounding St Patrick show an expertise in taking natural and pagan phenomena and presenting them in the garb of Christianity. The annual pilgrimage at the end of July when great throngs of supplicants make their painful way up the rough slopes of Croagh Patrick is reckoned to be a Christian adaptation of the pagan festival of Lughnasa, a hilltop celebration in summer of the Celtic god Lug. This extremely subtle process of grafting Christian values on to traditional customs and beliefs must have had much to do with the bloodless conversion which was achieved in Ireland. The countless springs, which were the focus of animistic worship stretching back over the millennia, were likewise all claimed for Christianity as holy wells. The old earth magic combined with the later religious sanctity of places such as St Patrick's Well near Clonmel in County Tipperary has an almost palpable quality. Here, an ancient cross has been set in the middle of a pond whose surface is alive with the countless swirls of underground water bubbling up. Also associated with the memory of St Patrick are the Struell Wells in County down where the spring is a unified source gushing forth and housed within some late medieval buildings. Patrick's legendary choice of the shamrock as Ireland's symbol of the Holy Trinity was truly inspired: for he showed it was possible, quite literally, to pluck a deep religious truth from an ordinary Irish meadow. And are the three circles of the shamrock somehow reminiscent of the triple spiral at Newgrange, an image still lurking deep in the folk-memory?

As for the plain facts of St Patrick's life, we have an account in the saint's own *Confessio* which tells how he was carried off from his home somewhere in Romanized Britain by Irish raiders and was forced to work as a swineherd for six long, unhappy years. The extinct volcanic hill known as Slemish in County Antrim is the traditionally accepted spot of Patrick's servitude. Then a voice prompted him to escape by ship to Gaul and thence home to his own people in Britain. Here he heard those memorable words, the voice of the Irish speaking 'as with

Struell Wells, Co. Down, are associated with St Patrick and have been a site of pilgrimage over many centuries.

one mouth': 'We beseech thee, holy youth, to come hither and walk among us.' This was the call which led Patrick to return to the place of his enforced exile and to spend the rest of his life converting the Irish people to Christianity.

According to the *Chronicle* of Prosper of Aquitaine, a certain Palladius was despatched by Pope Celestine in AD 431 to minister to 'those of the Irish who believed in Christ'. Who Palladius was or what he achieved is hard to tell, for there is no record of his doings in Ireland; but the reference to Christians already present among the Irish is clear enough. So Patrick did not confront an entirely pagan people. According to the Irish annals, Patrick's own mission commenced in the year 432 hard on the heels of that recorded for Palladius. Significantly, both men were appointed by the church authorities in Gaul. Whatever the exact circumstances, there is general accord that it was St Patrick who accomplished the comprehensive and enduring conversion of the Irish people.

Some say that he first landed at Strangford Lough near a place called Saul in County Down, where a local chieftain granted him a barn (Gaelic *sabhal*, which is pronounced 'saul') to be used as a church. The site is now marked by a church in the style of the Celtic Revival, built in 1932. But it was Armagh that Patrick declared should have pre-eminence over the other churches in Ireland; and so it has remained to this day both for the Roman Catholic Church and the Church of Ireland. Possibly Armagh, meaning 'Heights of Macha', was chosen to upstage the pagan shrine of Emain Macha (Navan Fort) only two miles away. Regardless of the prestige of Armagh, St Patrick was buried at Down Cathedral in the city of Downpatrick. In the graveyard there is a huge rock slab bearing the name of the saint, spelled as PATRIC, but this dates only from 1901. Furthermore, it could possibly mark the burial place of St Columba and St Brigid as well. Never mind that Iona claims the former and Kildare the latter, for the Norman

This grave at Down Cathedral, Downpatrick, is said to contain the bones of Ireland's three most revered saints.

Glencolumbkille, Co. Donegal; the holy well is an important station of the pilgrimage round performed on 9 June.

magnate John de Courcy maintained that he had interred the remains of all three of the greatest Irish saints in a single grave. And who would have dared to argue with the likes of John de Courcy?

Columba or Colmcille was certainly Ireland's most illustrious native saint, born in County Donegal in the year 522. The site of his birthplace is marked by a modern high cross above Lough Gartan. Columba was of royal blood and a fiery spirit in contradiction to his popular name in Irish meaning 'dove of the church'. He staunchly defended the threatened status of the bards and poets; and his militant qualities made him an ideal candidate to spread the Christian message into the Irish colony of Dalriada which was successfully expanding from its base in south-west Scotland. Arguably, Columba did more to merit the rank and title of patron saint of Scotland than St Andrew. Such was the Irish presence abroad at this time that it is more appropriate to think in terms of the Irish world rather than just the territory of Ireland. Irish saints and missionaries carried the Gospels with them into Scotland, Wales and Cornwall. Whatever debt Ireland may have owed to the larger island of Britain for transmitting Christianity was repaid with interest during Britain's Dark Ages when the pagan Saxons were conquering the land. During these years Ireland was a bright spiritual light in the west, despatching missionaries and keeping the faith alive. Some notable English monasteries were founded by Irish monks; the most resplendent was that at Lindisfarne in Northumbria, founded by St Aidan from the Columban community on Iona.

As a result of Columba's mission being devoted to Scotland, Ireland does not have too many Columban sites on her own soil; but the memory of the saint has been beautifully preserved in a valley by the sea in his native county of Donegal. Glencolumbkille is an enchanting place strewn with prehistoric as well as early Christian relics.

Colmcille's Chapel at Glencolumbkille is a reminder of St Columba's deeds in this remote part of County Donegal.

The *turas* or 'pilgrimage round' of St Columba takes in a fascinating collection of ancient stones inscribed with archaic crosses, the ruins of 'Colmcille's Chapel' and a well on the hillside decorated with an abundance of votive offerings. Nearby is Screig na Deamhan, or the 'Demons' Rock', where Columba expelled a last enclave of venomous creatures which, when driven away by St Patrick, hadn't left Ireland for good, but had taken refuge here in

St Brigid's Well near Kildare, a modern shrine to the most enduring guardian of Ireland's spiritual values.

the wild and remote north-west of the country. Thus did Columba follow in the footsteps of Patrick. Legend has it that Columba carried out this valuable service to his native land before setting sail for Iona in the year 565, dying there eventually in 597. His biographer Adamnan, a later abbot of Iona, described Columba's departure from Ireland as a sad experience, seeking out 'a solitude in the pathless sea', a sense of exile that has been shared by many Irish people down the centuries.

Adamnan's account delivers us a realistic picture of Columba as a well-documented historical personality; but with Brigid, the third supposed occupant of the saintly grave in Downpatrick, we are on less solid ground. Ireland's most popular female saint has received lavish treatment from later hagiographers, but there is more than a lingering suspicion that St Brigid has been created as a Christian version of the pagan Celtic triple-goddess of the same name. Indeed, it is certain that St Brigid's Day on the first of February took over from the time-hallowed, pre-Christian festival of Imbolc. Such is the ambivalence surrounding St Brigid that commentators are divided about whether to treat her as a clever fiction or as a person of flesh and blood who walked this earth from around the middle of the fifth century until her death in the year 525.

Whatever her precise origins, St Brigid's enormous popularity is beyond dispute. Kildare derived great prestige as the city of St Brigid, even to the extent that it threatened the primacy of Armagh for a while. When Gerald of Wales visited Kildare towards the end of the twelfth century, he reported the custom of a perpetual flame being tended by a community of nineteen nuns who each in turn spent a night in solitude by the fire to keep it burning. However, every twentieth night the fire was left untended and committed to the care of St Brigid, who never failed in her task. The site of the Sacred Fire is ascribed to a small building, situated to the north of the nave of Kildare Cathedral. Just outside the city lies St Brigid's Well, lovingly tended, where the latest manifestation of the elusive lady saint may be seen. Here we may gaze upon the image of the personage who may have begun life as a pagan goddess, now kitted out in the habit of a Roman Catholic nun.

The illustrious trio of Patrick, Columba and Brigid were, however, just three of many saints, holy men and women, who made Ireland such an influential and inspirational Christian country. St Patrick is credited with the ordination of as many as 400 bishops in line with the episcopal structure of the Church of Rome which was organized in territorial dioceses based on cities or centres of population. Since there were no proper towns in fifth-century Ireland it must be imagined that Patrick's bishops were attached to individual tribes or *tuatha*.

The Patrician conversion of Ireland took immediate root and flourished, but the structure of the early Irish church was rapidly adapted to Irish circumstances. The enthusiasm for the monastic ideas of Egypt and Syria spread through Europe and struck a sympathetic chord in the Irish soul. Soon the territorial administration of Christianity in Ireland through bishops faded away and was replaced by the authority of abbots in myriad monastic cells, mostly remote from human society where the light of the new faith could burn with greatest intensity. Thus the Irish monks scattered themselves all over the

This massive stone lintel at Fore, Co. Westmeath, is reputed to have been spirited into place by the powers of a saint.

countryside seeking out lonely and exposed places where they might pit their faith against the wild elements in a battle for survival. The age of anchorites, mystics and hermits was born; and the proliferation of early monastic sites, whose stirring relics may still be visited, is a lasting testimonial to Ireland's unique contribution in the context of Europe to a nascent Christianity.

Skellig Michael off the coast of Kerry is Europe's remotest and most spectacular outpost of Christianity.

A MULTITUDE OF MONKS

THE QUEST FOR solitude and austerity which was the guiding light of the early Irish monastic movement was easily satisfied by the topography of Ireland. There may have been no desert wastelands where a hermit might submit his faith and his life to the ultimate test, but there were numerous islands in the country's countless lochs as well as many offshore. The latter were close enough to be clearly visible but were remote by virtue of the dangerous waters which separated them from the mainland. All along the west coast of Ireland there was hardly a piece of rock in the ocean which was not claimed for the foundation of a monastery. Reputed to have been the first and with the severest regime was that at Killeany on the Aran island of Inishmore, founded early in the sixth century by St Enda, who had received his instruction at St Ninian's 'Candida Casa' at Whithorn in south-west Scotland. What remained of the monastery was finally destroyed in 1652 by the Cromwellian invaders who plundered its stone in order to construct a coastal fort. All that may be seen today is the base of a tower, once 80 feet high, a cross shaft and the saint's well nearby. Inishmore's hospitable bay at Kilronan made the island relatively accessible and vulnerable.

The same cannot be said of the jagged pinnacle of rock off the coast of County Kerry, a mountain peak protruding from the foaming Atlantic like the petrified tooth of some fearsome monster lurking beneath the waves. Great Skellig is the name of this western outpost of Ireland. Its even less welcoming neighbour is Small Skellig and together the pair have been described as 'two mighty ships, sailing along majestically with every shred of canvas set'. Perhaps the image is rather benign, but it does capture the dynamic essence of these two islets which defy anyone to set foot on them. The sheer cliffs of Small Skellig have ensured that it has remained the exclusive preserve of gannets and seals; Great Skellig offered no more than a toe-hold for human settlement but just enough to tempt the Irish monks to chance their luck. How many perished before one of their frail leather ships made a successful landfall can only be guessed at, and likewise the number who succumbed to the force of the waves over the centuries as new monks and essential supplies were ferried over.

Getting there was a physical achievement surpassed only by the building of Europe's most spectacular island monastery. Though modest in scale, the tiny settlement of six beehive cells and two oratories possesses a grandeur of spirit which takes the breath away. Dedicated to the Archangel Michael, the monastery of Sceilg Mhichil or Skellig Michael derives its awesome power to impress from the bold improbability of its situation, tenuously perched on a rocky shelf a 500-foot sheer drop above the

The Gallarus Oratory, Co. Kerry – a precious relic of early Christian architecture that has stood the test of time.

sea. The beehive huts, though outwardly round, provide a quadrangular living space within. The excellence of the construction shows that the monks had taken the trouble to acquire the skills of drystone masonry. The dwellings are still snug and weatherproof; and it is easy to imagine both the comfort and exhilaration to be experienced within during one of those violent storms when the Atlantic is whipped into full fury, and the salty spray can be tasted in the wind on the summit.

The regular visitation of death on the small community is movingly brought to mind by a simple cemetery filled with roughly hewn stone crosses. There is no place imaginable so exposed to both sea and sky which could be closer to the vast solitude of the universe. On the way up to the monastery there is a broad hump known as Christ's

Saddle; and from here the path ahead is a flight of stone steps up the mountainside, looking very much like a stairway to heaven.

The drystone construction technique of the beehive huts consists of oversailing courses gradually coming together. This method, known as corbelling, is a very ancient one and may be traced right back to the megalithic tomb at Newgrange. Skellig Michael is thus a direct descendant of the earliest tradition of Irish building, and one generally associated with monastic sites. Clusters of these characteristic *clochain* are particularly in evidence at several places along the Dingle Peninsula in County Kerry. Here one may also see corbelling applied to rectangular structures such as the famous Gallarus Oratory. This stone church looks uncannily like an upturned rowing boat. As you first peer through the inclined jambs and square lintel of its single doorway, it seems as gloomy as a cave inside; but as the eyes grow accustomed to the conditions so the internal light turns out to be much stronger and it is possible to admire the excellence of the stone engineering. But for all the mastery of technique, the rectangular corbelled building lacks the all-round stability of the circular beehives, and the roof sags gently amidships. A similar oratory at nearby Kilmalkedar has succumbed to this inherent design flaw.

The church on St Macdara's Island off the coast of Galway, founded originally by a sixth-century saint, is thought to be a later re-creation in stone of a previous wooden structure on the site. Indeed, the concept of 'petrified carpentry' offers us the best hope of reconstructing in the mind's eye the earlier generations of wooden churches which were the norm in Ireland between the fifth and eighth centuries. St Macdara's has recently been rebuilt from the tumbledown masonry, and it shows the unmistakable influence of the design technology of wooden buildings. The projecting antae are continued up into the gable and eventually cross over at the apex to form an attractive finial. As with early stone churches in general, it is impossible to ascribe anything like a precise date.

For an overall impression of an early Irish monastic settlement we must go to yet another island, that of Inishmurray off the coast of Sligo. The entire community was contained within an elliptical cashel, the stone wall surviving up to a maximum of 13 feet and penetrated by five entrances at various points. There are a number of beehive huts, similar to those of Skellig Michael, and three rectangular buildings, of which at least two were churches, showing the tendency to build several small churches rather than one of greater size. Perhaps the structural problems had not yet been overcome. Wood, on the other hand, did not suffer from the same limitations as stone. St Brigid's Church at Kildare was reputedly a magnificent affair, but like all the other wooden buildings of the period, it has fallen victim to the destructive forces of nature, in this case to fire rather than slow decay.

In order to form an idea of early monastic Ireland we must, however, think in terms of wood, wicker and thatch rather than of stone architecture. Such were the most common building materials even during the 'Golden Age' of the seventh and eighth centuries, when marvels of craftsmanship emerged in vast quantities from the workshops of the monks. Foremost among the ecclesiastical treasures of this period is the Ardagh Chalice, a magnificent silver vessel adorned with bronze and gold filigree. It is closely related to the exquisite Tara Brooch, one of many penannular ornaments designed for a decorative fastening of the Irish cloak. Both objects are now on permanent display in the National Museum of Ireland in Dublin.

Beside metalcraft, that other superlative skill of the early Irish monks was the illumination of manuscripts.

The interior of the Gallarus Oratory affords strong protection from the Atlantic winds which strafe the Dingle.

The old monastery of Kells, Co. Meath, gave its name to the miraculous Book of Kells, a masterpiece of c. AD *800.*

The often critical Gerald of Wales noted of the ancient decoration of the Gospels which he had seen at Kildare: 'If you take the trouble to look very closely, and penetrate with your eyes to the secrets of the artistry, you will notice such intricacies, so delicate and subtle that you will not hesitate to declare that all these things must have been the result of the work not of men but of angels.' Thus we may give credit to Gerald of Wales for coining the felicitous expression 'the work of angels' to characterize the whole range of crafts which resulted from the impetus given to Celtic design skills by the fresh breath of Christianity. Two of the most magnificent of the illuminated manuscripts, the Book of Durrow and the priceless Book of Kells, are displayed in the library of Trinity College in Dublin.

The complexities and artistry of the Book of Kells have occupied the analytical powers of several generations of art historians. Oriental inspiration, relayed via the monasteries of Europe, has been surmised; and the possibility is more plausible than at first apparent when one considers the extensive travels of the Irish monks who took their learning and religious perceptions to the centres of European culture during the time of Charlemagne and later. Heiric of Auxerre has given us a memorable report from the year 870: 'Almost all of Ireland, disregarding the sea, is migrating to our shores with a flock of philosophers.' Other commentators have remarked on the essentially Celtic manner of the decoration of the Book of Kells, with its curvilinear patterns and never a straight line when a curved one will do, and the taste for embellishing every last nook and cranny of the available space with some sort of motif. This cramming of design has been described in quasi-psychological terms as a fear of emptiness.

The Celtic inheritance was also noticeable in matters of church organization and customs. The Synod of Whitby had decided in the year 664 that the Irish must conform to

Devenish Island, Co. Fermanagh, has kept its round tower and its monastic aura inviolate from the modern world.

the standardized practice of the Church of Rome, especially with regard to the calculation of the date of Easter and the curious ear-to-ear tonsure of the Celtic monks which may have been a last remnant of druidic style. One may detect in the Synod of Whitby the first imposition of an alien system on the Irish, although it was one which traditionally minded Irish clerics could perhaps afford to ignore at least for the time being.

The Book of Kells also serves to remind us of the desperate social and political situation which developed

The round tower at Ardmore, Co. Waterford, is among the finest in Ireland, rising in three stages to ninety-five feet.

after the year 795 when the first of many bloody Viking raids unleashed terror and destruction on Ireland. It is thought that the Kells manuscript had been commenced by the Irish monks at the Columban foundation of Iona in the Inner Hebrides of Scotland, and that fear of the Vikings caused them to seek refuge in a daughter-house at Kells where the glorious illumination was completed.

Irish monasteries suffered most grievously at the hands of the Norsemen whose depravities are now being offset by historians who stress the later benefits which they brought to Ireland in terms of urbanism and international trade. But in the ninth century their very name struck fear and panic into the hearts of all. The monasteries on the remote islands posed no obstacle to these intrepid sea-farers. Even the redoubtable Skellig Michael was assaulted by the Vikings in 812 and again in 823 when the abbot Eitgal was taken prisoner and left to die of hunger and thirst, a punishment that was probably considered lenient by some of the marauders. Entire generations lived and died in a state of constant apprehension, as witnessed by this verse written in the margin of a ninth-century manuscript:

> Fierce and wild is the wind tonight,
> It tosses the tresses of the sea to white;
> On such a night as this I take my ease,
> Fierce Northmen only course the quiet seas.

The round towers characteristic of so many early Irish monasteries have been interpreted as look-out posts and refuges in the case of a Viking attack. Indeed, the placing of the solitary entrance door at a good height above the ground conjures up the image of monks scuttling to safety up a ladder which they would then withdraw behind them before bolting the door. But the Irish name for the round tower, *cloigtheach* meaning 'house of the bell', suggests a campanile of sorts, but certainly not one with a

The monastic site at Nendrum, Co. Down, is a scattering of ruins which include a church and the stump of a round tower.

large bell suspended, rather more likely a hand-bell rung by a single monk. The possibility has also been raised that the 'house of the bell' might even refer to the saint's bell of the founder which would have been the main treasure of any monastery.

Although the precise function of the round towers of Ireland has yet to be completely understood, a great deal is known about their method of construction. They all have a slight batter or tapering which greatly enhances their stability, which depends entirely on the strength of

St Kevin's Kitchen at Glendalough, Co. Wicklow, is a church that owes its name to the tower protruding like a chimney.

the outer shell of the building, for the internal floors were invariably of wood and communication between them was through trapdoors by ladder rather than fixed staircases. At Ardmore in County Waterford the internal organization is given external expression through a series of stylish string-courses, each one marking a further accentuation of the batter. The foundations for such weighty structures are surprisingly shallow, which speaks volumes for the skills of the masons. Inevitably, however, there have been some instances where the tower has settled down, creating an inclination. The most notable case of this is the round tower at Kilmacduagh in County Galway which is perceptibly out of true and has drawn the obvious comparisons to its more famous and endangered counterpart at Pisa.

This solitary example serves to underline the remarkably upright posture of the rest of Ireland's surviving round towers, which with their distinctive conical caps have all the rectitude of stone pencils jabbed into the landscape with immaculate precision. The round tower also constitutes a distinguished Irish contribution to international architecture. Though some writers have dismissed them as lacking in inspiration, any connoisseur of the genre will be quick to point out their sophisticated features such as that slight swelling of the contour, known to the Greeks as *entasis*, which counteracts the distortion of the perspective through height. Then there is the variety of lintels and the occasional decorative motifs such as the crucifixion carved over the entrance of the round tower at Donaghmore in County Meath and the attractive Romanesque doorway of four receding orders at Timahoe in County Laois. The dates of construction of the round towers span the tenth to the twelfth centuries, it is thought, but their presence always indicates the existence of a much earlier monastic site. Without exaggeration, they are one of the glories of Ireland, better experienced at scenic locations such as Devenish Island in County Fermanagh, rather than when engulfed by modern cities such as Kildare and Kilkenny.

Whether or not the round towers provided any effective defence against the Vikings is difficult to ascertain, but it does appear that the monasteries of Ireland were not always cast in the role of passive victims. There are records of Irish abbots sallying forth with armed men at their command. The Abbot of Terryglass and Clonenagh and the Deputy Abbot of Kildare both died a warrior's

The leaning tower of Kilmacduagh, Co. Galway, once surveyed an animated centre of religious activity.

89

Clonmacnoise, Co. Offaly, is the grandest of Ireland's monastic sites. Its present serenity belies a troubled past.

death in a battle against the Vikings fought in the year 845 near the mighty fortress of Dunamase. It should also be remembered that most monasteries were enmeshed in the chaotic tribal politics of the day and often suffered at the hands of their fellow countrymen in countless feuds and skirmishes. Yet such was the vigour of the monastic movement that not one foundation was expunged from the map during the period of the Viking raids. After each reverse there was a painful recovery and rebuilding, a fresh act of faith and a renewal of the spirit. The land of saints and scholars was not to be subdued by force of arms.

The monasteries signified more than a purely religious phenomenon. Some of the larger establishments amounted to veritable cities; and they constituted the first sizeable centres of population in Ireland before towns as such came into being when the Vikings turned from raiders into settlers and laid the foundations of the future cities of Dublin, Waterford, Wexford and Limerick. When visiting the larger of the early monastic sites such as Clonmacnoise and Glendalough it should be remembered that these now deserted places were once buzzing with human activity and were home to thousands of people.

The remains at Glendalough, covering several centuries of occupation, are strewn over a distance of one and a half miles in a picturesque wooded valley in the Wicklow Hills. The place, whose Irish name means 'Glen of the Two Lakes', was chosen by St Kevin in the year 570 for the site of his monastery. Kevin belonged to the hermitic breed of monks, and when he first came to Glendalough he lived for a while in the hollow of a tree'. He left but returned later to take up permanent residence in a beehive hut now known as St Kevin's Cell. St Kevin's Bed, a cave in the rock-face some 25 feet above the lake, was reputedly his retreat for spiritual solitude. The saintliness of Kevin's example attracted many admirers who wished to associate themselves with him; and in the course of time the hermit found himself the nucleus of a monastic community which continued to flourish and expand in the centuries after his death.

The extant buildings at Glendalough date from the later period of the monastery. St Kevin's Church, sometimes referred to as his kitchen on account of the small round tower attached suggesting a chimney, could be eleventh- or twelfth-century; and likewise the Cathedral and St Saviour's Priory. St Mary's Church could go back to the tenth century, and so too could the 100-foot-high round tower whose conical roof was rebuilt with the original stones in 1876. The mystical antiquity of the site is greatly enhanced by the profusion of primitive stone crosses which reflect the simplicity and austerity of the monastery's beginnings.

Equally impressive, though in a totally different setting on a flat plain by a lazy bend of the lower reaches of the Shannon, is Clonmacnoise in County Offaly. It was founded by St Ciaran, who had once been a pupil of St Enda on Aran and subsequently a hermit on Hare Island in Lough Ree. Clonmacnoise was destined to suffer more than most from the depredations of the Vikings. Between the years 834 and 1204 it was plundered six times and burned twenty-six times, disaster striking on average every eleven and a half years. The Normans maintained the tradition with their attack in 1179 during which more than a hundred houses were burned to the ground; and so it continued throughout the Middle Ages at regular intervals until finally in 1552 the English garrison from Athlone carted off all the movable treasure and sounded the death-knell of the place.

Clonmacnoise has thus suffered more violence than many a battle-scarred castle, but somehow the sanctity of the site has come through it all, seemingly inviolate. Among all the many early monasteries of Ireland it exudes the most tangible atmosphere of spirituality which succeeds in dispelling all bad memories of past sufferings, including that inflicted by the Viking Turgesius who sought to desecrate the hallowed ground by planting his wife on the high altar to deliver a spate of pagan oracles. Most of the surviving remains are later than this calculated outrage, including those magnificent high crosses and carved slabs which make Clonmacnoise the best place in Ireland to embark on the discovery of these masterpieces of early Irish sculpture.

Muiredach's Cross at Monasterboice, Co. Louth, is a picture book in stone, carved more than a thousand years ago.

ART OF THE HIGH CROSS

THOUGH NOT UNIQUELY Irish, the idea of the sculptured high cross was brought to such a state of excellence in Ireland during the tenth century that it may be considered as another national symbol to set alongside the round tower. Standing stones, albeit unhewn and unadorned, were something of an Irish tradition from the Bronze Age; and rare glimpses of artistic carving can be gained at Neolithic Newgrange or the Iron Age decorated stones at Turoe and Castlestrange. But what emerged in the Christian era was something totally new and exciting. With the advent of Christianity the way was open for the symbolism of the cross to spark off a fresh artistic vision which had no obvious roots in the past. At first the design consisted of little more than a carving of the cross itself on a roughly shaped pillar stone or slab. The splendid example at Fahan Mura in County Donegal from the seventh century presents us with an elaborately executed cross composed of delicate interlacing curved lines which seem related to the illuminated manuscripts of the period.

From this point there was no continuous development of the art but rather a quantum leap to arrive centuries later at the almost architectural splendour of the imposing high crosses such as Muiredach's Cross at Monasterboice in County Louth or the Cross of the Scriptures at Clonmacnoise in County Offaly. The name of the latter reflects what was certainly the essential didactic purpose of these crosses, namely to relate in a durable, three-dimensional form the teachings and stories of the Bible. These storybooks in stone were an ideal medium for the almost wholly illiterate public of the time, and they possessed the added advantage that they were too heavy to be carried off by the Vikings.

In like fashion to the manuscript illuminators, the sculptors of the high crosses appear to have been driven by an overriding need to decorate every available surface. The figurative sculpture when at its best is of the highest order; but even the simpler work such as the depiction of the twelve apostles rather like identical pawns in a chess set on the base of the Moone Cross in County Kildare has a charm of its own. At Dysert O'Dea in County Clare the compartmentalization has given way to a strong and naturalistic portrayal of a cleric on the shaft of the cross. Somewhere along the line the art of sculpting in stone had been acquired and perfected; and we still marvel at the beauty of technique and conception, though the carvings are dulled by the passage of about a thousand years. We can only guess at the effect these great and imposing works had when they first emerged, fresh and crisp from the sculptor's chisel.

The east face of the shaft of Muiredach's Cross shows many scenes from the Old Testament including Cain slaying Abel.

The Cross of the Scriptures at Clonmacnoise, Co. Offaly, stands directly in front of the ruined cathedral.

The interlace pattern of this cross at Ahenny, Co. Tipperary, has been likened to the decoration of the Book of Kells.

The shaft of the cross at Dysert O'Dea, Co. Clare, is taken up by this striking effigy of a bishop of the twelfth century.

Adam and Eve are at the centre of this imposing series of Romanesque carvings at Ardmore, Co. Waterford.

A ROMANESQUE REVOLUTION

ONE OF THE MOST significant single acts in the emerging Christian identity of Ireland was the granting in 1101 by Muirchertach of the royal mound of the Kings of Munster to the Church. The mound in question, known as the Rock of Cashel, is thus a symbol of a significant shift in values; but for a while temporal and religious leadership resided in the one person of Cormac Mac Carthaigh who was both King of Desmond and Bishop of Cashel. This was the man who commissioned the church between 1127 and 1134, familiarly known as Cormac's Chapel, which has been acclaimed by some as Ireland's first major work of architecture.

It is difficult now to appreciate the full splendour of Cormac's Chapel since the building of the thirteenth-century Gothic cathedral alongside severely impinged on its space, so that it is hemmed in on the north and the west. The aspect of the south front was not improved by the insertion of two rectangular windows. Nevertheless, this architectural gem marks the full-blooded arrival in Ireland of the mature Romanesque style. The round arches of the north and south doors and of the blind arcading on the internal and external walls were the hallmark of the Romanesque which had already spread across Britain with the advance of the conquering Normans. However, Cormac's Chapel was well ahead of the arrival of the Norman barons in Ireland and it shows that the country was keeping abreast of European trends.

Not surprisingly, this prominent and exotic creation was imitated elsewhere in Ireland. Although none of its emulators seriously challenged the sophistication of Cormac's Chapel, there did occur a widespread move away from the heavy, square lintels of the typical early Christian doorway to the round arch of the Romanesque, which offered plenty of scope for the decorative fantasies of the Irish sculptors.

Pleasing examples of this Hiberno-Romanesque may be seen at Ardmore in County Waterford and at Kilmalkedar in County Kerry; and within the nineteenth-century Tuam Cathedral in County Galway there is a splendid chancel arch of the twelfth century. The style reached its height during the 1160s with Clonfert Cathedral in County Galway and the Nun's Church at Clonmacnoise in County Offaly. The west door of Clonfert Cathedral is a spectacular affair. Its six orders of recessed arches are Romanesque enough, but the columns on which they rest are inclined in the manner of the earlier tradition. Rising at a tangent to the curve of the outermost arch are two linear mouldings which soar to meet at a point to create a triangular shape that is reminiscent of the gable end of the first Irish stone churches. Within this space are arrayed a bizarre collection of human heads, possibly a reference to an ancient pagan cult.

The twelfth-century doorway at Kilmalkedar on the Dingle Peninsular, Co. Kerry, is typical of Hiberno-Romanesque.

The west door of Clonfert Cathedral, Co. Galway, comprises an astounding array of motifs including human heads.

The Nun's Church at Clonmacnoise is a fine example of the nave and chancel type. It was completed in 1166.

The Nun's Church at Clonmacnoise is also disturbing in its imagery, with fearsome beasts on the capitals of the west door, but the overall effect of this roofless nave-and-chancel church is rather pleasing. The chancel arch is lavishly decorated and well lit in its exposed situation. Interestingly, this is the burial place of Dervorgilla, wife of Tighernan O'Rourke of Breffny, the lady who was scandalously abducted by Dermot Mac Murrough. Dermot ranks as the most treacherous of Irishmen on account of his appeal to Henry II of England to intervene on his behalf against the High King of Ireland, Rory O'Connor, who had banished him. This shameful internal feud was to provide the pretext for an Anglo-Norman invasion; and so the Nun's Church at Clonmacnoise, to which Dervorgilla retired as a penitent in 1170 in the aftermath of the military intervention, provides more than a lesson in architectural history.

Sunset at Dunluce Castle, Co. Antrim – a most spectacular fortification perched on the very edge of a rugged cliff.

STRONGHOLDS OF STONE

ACCORDING TO THE much-quoted Gerald of Wales who travelled extensively in Ireland in the wake of the Anglo-Norman invasion, the Irish 'have no use for castles. Woods are their forts and swamps their ditches.' The idea of the 'wild Irish' living a primitive existence amidst the bogs and forests of their native land was one that persisted, at least in the reports of English observers, throughout the Middle Ages. Certainly, by the standards of the invaders, the scattered raths were more like cattle corrals than anything resembling castellated comfort; and it would seem that the Irish chieftains did not lay much importance on sophisticated strongholds of stone for themselves and their families. Given the frequency of raids and rustling, there was much virtue in remaining mobile and flexible. What point was there, when so much of life was spent roaming the land, and attacks were an endemic risk to property and fixed assets, of exposing oneself in a permanent and expensive abode? However, to suggest that the Irish were unable to build adequate defences is clearly wrong, when the enduring evidence of ring-forts such as Dun Aengus and the Grianán of Aileach is taken into account.

Nevertheless, the idea of the fortified residence of stone, which has left such an indelible mark on the Irish landscape, was a direct contribution of the Anglo-Norman invaders, whose conquest was made much easier by the lack of any native fortifications of substance as well as by widespread internecine strife. The heroic victory of Brian Boru over the Norsemen in 1014 at the Battle of Clontarf had not led to any consolidation of royal authority over a united nation. The Kingdom of Leinster had been the ally of the Vikings; and it was a deposed King of Leinster, Dermot Mac Murrough, who invited the Anglo-Normans to intervene in a land that was no stranger to the ravages of war. 'There has been fighting in all provinces, endless campaigns, burnings, atrocities – Ireland lies like a trembling sod.' So ran a contemporary account.

Interestingly, the first wave of land-hungry and mercenary barons were from Wales rather than England itself, so that the initial stages could be better described as a Cambro-Norman invasion; and the first victims of the invasion were the citizens of Wexford, predominantly of Viking stock. Since the Normans themselves were only a few generations removed from their Norse mother-country, it can be claimed that the opening scene of the Anglo-Norman hostilities against Ireland was essentially a Scandinavian affair.

The castle was a symbolic and physical act of consolidation by the new occupying powers. In the early stages it was a hasty, transient affair, a 'motte' or mound of earth piled high, with a timber palisade to protect the garrison. Sometimes an attached area enclosed within a bank,

Trim Castle, Co. Meath. The site was fortified in 1172 by Hugh de Lacy, but the castle was not completed until 1220.

known as a 'bailey', was appended. All the timber structures have long since decayed back into the soil, but the mounds remain. Simple though they look, they represent thousands of man-hours, probably of conscripted labour. Ireland is liberally peppered with these mounds, now bare and mute, relics of the first wave of the conquest. Granard in County Longford and Knockgraffon in County Tipperary are imposing examples of the type.

The structure reputed to be the very first Norman stronghold in Ireland, erected in 1169–70 by Robert Fitzstephen after the capture of Wexford, now finds itself conveniently located as an exhibit within the confines of the Irish National Heritage Park at Ferrycarrig in County Wexford. Although the fortification was described as but 'a flimsy wall of branches and sods' it was sufficiently strong to enable a handful of men to hold out against a determined counter-attack by a large force of local people. The eventual surrender of Fitzstephen and his companions was brought about not by force but by a clever subterfuge.

Until great castles of stone could be built, there was a large window of vulnerability through which the invaders could contemplate the Irish all about them. Trim Castle in County Meath was destined to be the largest bastion of Norman power in Ireland, but in its first guise as a 'motte and bailey' it was not very effective. In 1173, just one year after it was finished, it was stormed and taken by the King of Connaught; and for a while the place was abandoned. However, native resistance turned out in the long run to be fitful and sporadic, so that the stone castle was eventually consolidated. The present mighty ruins date from the rebuilding which occurred between 1210 and 1220. This pile of scarred masonry still dominates the town of Trim, but its once threatening presence has been somewhat reduced since the area around the castle wall has become the preserve of the local pitch and putt club.

Dundrum Castle, Co. Down, was founded by John de Courcy around 1177, but it passed in 1227 to the Earls of Ulster.

The massive keep at Trim, four-square and with walls 11 feet thick, was not the blueprint for all other castles in Ireland: for it had been discovered that right-angled corners could easily be undermined by sappers. The cylindrical keep at Dundrum in County Down thus marks an advance in military architecture. The castle was begun by John de Courcy soon after his arrival in Ireland in 1177, but the circular 'donjon' was probably the work of his

Carrickfergus Castle, Co. Antrim, was the scene of bloody sieges by King John in 1210 and by Edward Bruce in 1315.

successors, the Earls of Ulster, who held Dundrum following his expulsion from Ulster in 1204.

Carrickfergus in County Antrim was one of the earliest of the great stone castles of Ireland; and it ranks among the best preserved of its period. It was also begun by the enterprising John de Courcy, but he lost it to his arch-rival Hugh de Lacy, another ambitious Anglo-Norman magnate. It was not just the Irish who fought among themselves. Indeed, Hugh de Lacy soon became too powerful as Earl of Ulster and found himself being cut down to size by King John who besieged and captured Carrickfergus Castle in 1210. Hugh de Lacy's mighty, square keep still maintains a watchful eye on the waters of Belfast Lough. The stonework of this castle is worth inspecting at close quarters, for it shows a splendid range of colours from sandstone browns with a shot of red or purple to limestone yellow and basalt black. Perhaps the most dramatic incident in the career of the castle was the siege by the Scottish king, Robert Bruce. This dragged on for over a year; and the defending garrison fended off starvation by dining on the remains of some of their Scottish prisoners who had expired.

Roscommon Castle in the county of the same name was a royal possession from the start. It represented an attempt by the Crown to assert its authority and to impose order on the unruly remoter reaches of the country. The King of Connaught, Hugh O'Conor, launched a series of fierce attacks soon after building had begun in 1270, and more than once he succeeded in demolishing the work in progress. Once again, Anglo-Norman determination wore down the resolve of the opposition; and gradually Roscommon Castle made its defiant appearance on land which had been grabbed from the Dominican friars. The present aspect of the castle is due partly to the new fenestration of 1578 and to subsequent dismantling of the defences by the Cromwellians in 1652.

Roscommon Castle was a Norman foundation, but it changed hands several times in the course of the Middle Ages.

Significantly, the O'Conors of Connaught who held Roscommon for a while were so impressed that they used it as a model for their own royal castle built nearby at Ballintober, County Roscommon. Four splendid polygonal towers and an imposing curtain wall enclosed a rectangular courtyard of princely dimensions and stately apartments. Now all is ivy-clad oblivion and overgrown abandon; but this was once a unique, magnificent gesture by an Irish king to signal that princely castles were not the exclusive prerogative of the Anglo-Normans.

On the surface the profusion of castles might be taken as evidence of the Anglo-Norman take-over of Ireland. Individually, they indicate a great tenacity of purpose; and there is no doubt that the new lords and barons were resolved to stay indefinitely. However, the conquest was to remain incomplete and strangely inconclusive. The thrust of the invasion was lost at a very early date when Strongbow, Earl of Pembroke, who had acquired the Kingdom of Leinster through his marriage to the daughter of Dermot Mac Murrough, died without an heir. No pre-eminent Hiberno-Norman dynasty emerged to establish a united country. Direct intervention by the English monarchs from Henry II to Richard II did not succeed in settling the destiny of what was grandly known as the Lordship of Ireland, an autonomous entity but subject to the Crown.

For their part, the Irish did not take advantage of the lack of a coherent English policy but wasted too much energy pursuing their own quarrels to take effective issue with the invaders. But perhaps the most significant fact is that after a very short while the invaders no longer behaved quite like the representatives of a foreign power. They took personal control of large swathes of territory as individuals driven by selfish ambition, not as the obedient instruments of colonial policy. Many of the Anglo-Normans assimilated to a remarkable degree, showing a linguistic ability that today's Englishmen might envy, learning Irish and immersing themselves in the culture and history of Ireland. They identified with the folklore and patronized the Irish bards and poets. They intermarried and adopted local customs such as the fostering out of their own children. Very soon they became a race apart, a sort of middle nation, neither English nor yet Irish, but something in between. At the same time others

Cahir Castle, Co. Tipperary. A fine portcullis still hangs at this stronghold of the Butler Earls of Ormonde.

retreated into a different role as guardians of English values, and came to be known as the Old English in Ireland.

The extent to which some of the Anglo-Normans had gone native may be gauged from the Statutes of Kilkenny of 1366, which formally placed an interdict on the Gaelicization of the incomers in customs, games and language: 'if any English or Irish living amongst the English use the Irish language amongst themselves contrary to this ordinance and thereof be attaint, that his lands and tenements if he have any, be seized into the hands of his immediate lord.' It was even a libellous offence to call an Englishman an Irishman. But this imposition of a cultural apartheid came clearly too late. According to the famous saying of those times, the Anglo-Irish were already more Irish than the Irish. Just how far linguistic assimilation had gone may be seen from the case of one William Power who was sent to gaol in Waterford in 1371 'because he could not speak English'. He was released on payment of a fine of forty silver pence and an undertaking that he would 'apply himself diligently to learning English'. Thus to add to the confusion of national identity we have the curious phenomenon of non-Anglophone Englishmen. Knowing where you belonged and which side you were on became increasingly complex and flexible.

It was a sign of the times that the ancestor of one of the great Hiberno-Norman families, the Butler Barons of Cahir, was known as Seamus Gallda – 'James the Foreigner'. Cahir Castle in County Tipperary was his stronghold, the most imposing Irish castle of the early fifteenth century. It is thought that its redoubtable defences were intended against not the native Irish but the rival branch of the Butlers, the Earls of Ormonde as well as against the Fitzgerald Earls of Desmond. Such localized conflicts were the norm, so that the study of Irish medieval history is

The wall-stair at Cahir Castle is an evocative relic of medieval castle architecture that is still in good repair.

Battle-scarred Adare Castle watches over the River Maigue in mute testimony to the turbulence of the past.

rather like entering a trackless forest with numerous bogs to trap the unwary. In this shapeless world we cling to the castles as bastions of meaning, indicators of some sort of social or political structure, strategic signposts which tell us who ruled and held sway over a specific territory. Yet the reality was as restless and changing as the Irish weather sweeping in fitful moods across the country.

In this sense, the present state of abandoned castles such as Adare in County Limerick, mouldering away by the lovely banks of the River Maigue, is a fitting symbol of the very real vicissitudes of life in medieval Ireland. This castle was recorded to have been in ruins as early as the 1330s, and to have suffered again after partial reconstruction before the fourteenth century had run its course. The Cromwellians contributed their customary slighting in the mid-seventeenth century. The result is a tumbledown agglomeration of romantic masonry which conveys more of the authentic feel of history than many a modernized medieval castle.

The Anglo-Norman sphere of influence which still identified strongly with England shrank in the centuries after the invasion into a very narrow segment of territory. Rather like the Latin kingdoms of the Crusaders in Palestine, so the Anglo-Norman domains in Ireland also melted away, until they amounted to no more than a tenuous enclave around Dublin, known as the 'Pale', which extended inland a mere 30 miles. However, in its dominant role as the prime commercial town in Ireland Dublin had become a more important fact of Irish life than the old royal mounds of Tara and Cashel. The new world of international trade and urban administration had rendered obsolete the traditional notions of kingship. Being a monarch entailed the control of the levers of economic power, rather than the maintenance of a fanciful vision vaguely perceived through the sentimental mists of time. Dublin and the 'Pale' were thus more important than their territorial extent might suggest; and every effort was made to keep them intact by the erection of a new generation of castles. These were not great, strategic fortresses but fortified farmsteads, the bristling forward defences of a community that felt itself to be under siege. Its feeling of separate identity from the 'wild Irish' who were quite 'beyond the Pale' has given the English language an image that is still in use, though no longer generally understood.

The proliferation of neat tower-houses in the counties

Donore Castle, Co. Meath, is one of the many '£10 castles' built in the fifteenth century to defend the Pale.

Aughnanure Castle, Co. Galway, was built by the O'Flahertys in the early sixteenth century. The tower is six storeys high.

of the Pale is a noticeable feature of the area even today. The process was stimulated by a measure announced by Henry VI in 1429 which offered a £10 subsidy towards the building of a castle in the 'Pale' conforming to the dimensions of 20 feet long, 16 feet wide and 40 feet high. The response to the initiative was so strong that a rash of '£10' castles mushroomed in the counties of Dublin, Kildare, Louth and Meath. There were so many claimants of the subsidy in Meath that in 1449 limits on the number of castles in that county were imposed. The three-storey Donore Castle is a perfect specimen of the genre. Ironically, the idea of the tower-house as a secure home in troubled times caught on with the native Irish outside the Pale, who made it in a manner of speaking their own creation. Some four hundred in County Limerick and three hundred in County Cork have been identified.

For several centuries the tower-house was the most favoured residence of Irish noblemen great and small. It could be as imposing as Bunratty Castle in County Clare, commenced around 1450 by a certain Maccon MacSioda Macconmara whose splendid name amounts to a family tree in its own right. The equally imposing Blarney Castle in County Cork is another famous tower of similar vintage. At Dunguaire in County Galway may be found a delightful smaller version which was built in the 1520s on a rocky outcrop at Kinvara on the site of the sea-girt, seventh-century stronghold of the King of Connaught, Guaire Aidhne. His legendary reputation for hospitality and charity was so great that his right arm was said to be longer than his left from handing out gold to the poor. Dunguaire's picturesque coastal location, excellent restoration and the survival of its enclosure or 'bawn' make it a splendid example of the Irish tower-house.

Equally fascinating is Aughnanure Castle, also in County Galway, on the shores of Lough Corrib. This is a six-storey tower with machicolated parapets built by the O'Flahertys

Kilclief Castle, Co. Down, was the work of the Bishop of Down between 1413 and 1441. It has some fine machicolation.

around 1500. It is remarkable for having preserved both an inner and an outer 'bawn', each with elegant turrets in the south-west corner. Kilclief Castle in County Down is somewhat earlier, reputedly built by a Bishop of Down, John Sely, between 1413 and 1441. The main front is dominated by a majestic arch spanning the recess between the two projecting towers. This was not just for aesthetic reasons, but to drop missiles through the machicolation on any unwanted guests. Many of the tower-houses that are still inhabited have had larger windows installed, but this has falsified their appearance, as we may tell from the notes of a French traveller in Ireland in 1644, Monsieur Le Gouz de la Boullaye: 'The castles or houses of the nobility consist of four walls extremely high, thatched with straw; but to tell the truth, they are nothing but square towers without windows, or at least having such small apertures as to give no more light than a prison.'

The Irish tower-house fits into the chronology of rural lifestyle in Ireland as the medieval successor to the rath or ring-fort and the precursor of the country house. In political terms it may be seen as the type of stronghold favoured by all the opposing factions in Ireland during the Middle Ages when each tower-house was in a very real sense a protection against the occupants of other tower-houses. And herein lies their collective weakness. Individually sound and solid, robust and enduring, yet their very existence speaks of the tragic fragmentation of Irish society into a patchwork of personal, local and regional interests, a failing which was to make Ireland extremely vulnerable in face of the more organized and purposeful attempts at colonization which were soon to be launched from Tudor and Stuart England.

Ennis Friary, Co. Clare. Christ rises from the grave in one of the splendid panels of the Mac Mahon tomb.

DEATHLY DESIGNS

A S IF IN DEFIANCE of the Anglo-Norman invasion Gaelic Ireland looked deeper into its own roots for hope and inspiration, and traditional culture continued to thrive. However, in the visual art of stone sculpture we see a rather different process in action. Native artists absorbed the lessons from the wider realm of Anglo-Norman civilization and then applied their own genius to the discipline of figurative carving which had lain dormant since the era of those magnificent high crosses in the tenth century.

An exploration of medieval Ireland provides a precious personal encounter with the prolific output of the gifted Irish masons, above all through the medium of the newly fashionable sculptured tombs commissioned by the nobility and persons of rank. One of the delights of the effigies resides in the rich visual artistry of the canopied tomb-chests, where every opportunity was taken to give expression to a resonant religious faith. Some portrayals of Christ and the Apostles could well have been modelled on real people and are the most moving to be seen anywhere. But there are also portraits of bishops along with the knights and chieftains, which afford us a veritable face-to-face encounter with the actual personalities of medieval Ireland. The commemoration of the dead may provide the context for this sculptural flowering, but these deathly designs are very much a living human testimony which still speaks out across the centuries.

This priestly Benediction is another fine piece of figurative sculpture on display at Ennis Friary.

Effigy of a bishop sculpted in stone in the twelfth-century cathedral at Kilfenora, Co. Clare.

The over-life-size effigy of Thomas de Cantwell in Kilfane Church, Co. Kilkenny, dates back to the early Middle Ages.

The glorious sixteenth-century tomb of Piers Fitz Oge Butler at Kilcooly Abbey, Co. Tipperary, is marvellously carved.

Jerpoint Abbey, Co. Kilkenny, possesses some superb tomb-chests with representations of saints and apostles.

The sculptural quality of the carvings at Jerpoint is as potent and exciting as when freshly executed.

Detail of a tomb-chest at Strade Friary, Co. Mayo, of c. 1475 shows two of the Magi and Christ displaying his wounds.

The south transept of St Canice's Cathedral, Kilkenny, is like an Ormonde mausoleum. Here lies the 8th earl with his wife.

Knockmoy Abbey, Co. Galway. The north wall of the chancel displays some of the best medieval frescoes in Ireland.

CISTERCIAN SYMPHONY

'JOINING THE CLUB' – this view of a historian surveying the Anglo-Norman invasion of Ireland from a twentieth-century armchair strikes a detached note, suggesting perhaps that it was all for the best in that it connected Ireland to the wider sphere of European civilization which had already engulfed most of Britain. Without doubt the armed incursion into Irish affairs by Strongbow and company in the 1170s did open the way for a new political reality to make inroads into the Celtic fabric, but that does not mean that Ireland had previously been completely out of touch with the new Europe. Far from it, in fact, for some aspects of European culture had already been imported, and quite without the assistance of the Anglo-Norman barons. The ecclesiastical leaders of Ireland had 'gone into Europe' of their own free will some thirty years before the military intervention.

It was the pious St Malachy of Armagh who saw the pressing need to reform the old Celtic monasteries which had fallen by the wayside since the days of the founding fathers. All manner of lax practices were rampant: the law of celibacy was openly disregarded, and the office of abbot often passed to the issue of such irregular unions. The monasteries had become inextricably linked to their neighbouring tribes, so that they were entwined in all the local disputes, dissensions and even conflicts. Of course,

saintly Irish monks had not vanished from the face of the earth, and there must have been many among the estimated two hundred communities still true to the original vision. But the abuses were serious enough to cause St Malachy to take drastic action.

It was in the course of a journey through France in 1140 that he discovered at first hand the bracing reformist ideals of the Cistercians through the person of St Bernard at Clairvaux; and it was with his support that in 1142 St Malachy took the bold step of founding Ireland's first Cistercian monastery in County Louth. Even its name, Mellifont, was a striking novelty, introducing the Latin *fons mella* or 'fount of honey' into the world of Irish places. The choice of the Cistercians seemed to be an inspired one with its potent appeal to that ancient purity of spirit which had guided the early Irish Christians. Celtic monks figured prominently among the first recruits to the order who were instructed under the supervision of Cistercian brethren sent over from France. The decline of the nearby Celtic establishment of Monasterboice was directly linked to the rise of Mellifont. Very soon the process was repeated elsewhere as daughter-houses proliferated. Mellifont sounded the death-knell for traditional Irish monasticism, but it signified a triumphant rebirth of the monastic spirit.

Irish kings and chieftains were quick to associate themselves with the Cistercians. By 1170 four of Ireland's five provincial kings had come forward as patrons of the order, and there were perhaps as many as five hundred Cistercian monks distributed throughout Ireland's eleven foundations. At the consecration of Mellifont in 1157 Queen Dervorgilla, as yet unsullied by the advances of Dermot Mac Murrough, donated a golden chalice and 60 ounces of fine gold to help launch the establishment. It was an auspicious beginning.

The Cistercians proved to be a revolutionary force in Ireland. As agricultural pioneers they were industrious and effective tamers of the landscape. Gerald of Wales noted of their Irish endeavours: 'Give the Cistercians a wilderness or a forest, and in a few years you will find a dignified abbey in the midst of smiling plenty.' But it was as architects that they excelled, spreading Ireland's own 'great white robe of churches' in emulation of those of the Île de France. St Malachy's first building project had been at Bangor in County Down where he had encouraged the Augustinians to settle; and he had replaced the wooden church with one of stone. Not, it would seem, with the approval of all concerned, since we are told that one critic carped at Malachy: 'Good sir, why have you thought good to introduce this novelty into our regions? We are Irish not French. What is this frivolity? What need was there for a work so superfluous, so proud?' Unfortunately, no trace remains of Malachy's controversial stone church at Bangor; and it is not known if there were other dissenting voices as a host of stately stone churches sprouted up all over the Irish countryside.

Nor is there much to be seen of the church at Mellifont Abbey itself. A tantalizing fragment of an octagonal two-storey 'lavabo' or washing-house and a reconstructed portion of the Romanesque cloister arcade are the main features that strike the eye, along with the vaulted

Mellifont Abbey, Co. Louth – a fragment of the cloister at Ireland's first Cistercian house, founded in 1142.

fourteenth-century chapter house. As for the church itself, it is much ruined and some effort is required to imagine the dramatic effect it had when newly built. There is more visual satisfaction to be had by visiting some of the many daughters of Mellifont. These range from the heavy and austere cylindrical columns of Boyle Abbey in County Roscommon to the elegantly decorated stonework of Corcomroe Abbey in County Clare. This abbey was given the enticing name of 'St Mary of the Fertile Rock' because it sits by a patch of lush pasture, quite unexpected in the rugged, exposed rock terrain of the Burren. This remote spot perfectly evokes the mood of the early Cistercians, living on the very fringes of human society. In a more pastoral setting in County Galway, Knockmoy Abbey combines austerity in its nave with ornate finesse in its rib-vaulted chancel, giving a preview of how Cistercian architectural reticence was later to be abandoned, and with spectacular results. In all, the prolific family of Mellifont came to embrace some twenty-two monastic establishments in Ireland.

This was indeed an abundant 'fount of honey' as the name so clearly suggests, but the beguiling image should not deceive us into assuming that all at Mellifont was sweetness and light. There was from the outset a cultural clash between the French monks and the Irish that went beyond the merely linguistic. It was the Celtic character perhaps which was ill-suited to the rigid discipline and mind-numbing routine of the order. The way of the Cistercians has been vividly described by Ailred of Rievaulx: 'Our food is scanty, our garments rough, our drink is from the stream and our sleep often upon our book. Under our tired limbs there is but a hard mat; when sleep is sweetest, we must rise at bell's bidding. Self-will has no place; there is no moment for idleness or dissipation.' Conceivably, many of the Irish recruits were men of the people, reluctant to distance themselves from the normal

The octagonal lavabo at Mellifont once contained a fountain where the monks would wash their hands before meals.

Inch Abbey, Co. Down, was founded in the 1180s by John de Courcy in atonement for the despoliation of Erenagh.

run of life and to espouse the self-imposed rigour required by the Cistercians. At any rate, a ruction occurred very soon after Mellifont's foundation in 1142 which resulted in the return of the French contingent to Clairvaux, vowing never to set foot in Ireland again.

A further complication followed in the wake of the Anglo-Norman invasion, when French became associated not only with the Cistercians but also with the Francophone knights who were fighting the native Irish rulers who had founded the monasteries. The religious world found itself suddenly engulfed in a wider political conflict of interests; and this was confounded by the setting up of what amounted to a rival chain of Cistercian monasteries by the Anglo-Normans. These show how an uneasy conscience can be a great stimulus to performing acts of religious piety. Some of the warriors with the most blood on their hands turned out to be the most enthusiastic founders of abbeys. The swashbuckling John de Courcy, when he was not building castles or destroying abbeys, took time off to found Inch Abbey in County Down as a penance for his despoliation of Erenagh Abbey three miles to the south. Through his wife Affreca he also founded Grey Abbey in the same county. These establishments were totally imported productions, designed, built and eventually manned by masons and monks from England. Architecturally, they stand out as exponents of Early English Gothic, the austere unadorned phase of the style which is so closely associated with the ideals of the Cistercians. Only the magnificent west door of Grey Abbey would seem to go beyond the strict teachings of St Bernard.

Other Anglo-Norman contributions to Ireland's fast-growing inventory of Cistercian abbeys include Tintern in County Wexford and Graiguenamanagh in County Kilkenny. The latter was to be the largest of the Cistercian houses in Ireland. Its vast complex of domestic buildings

The west door at Grey Abbey, Co. Down, is a bold feature of the monastery founded in 1193 by de Courcy's wife, Affreca.

has since been invaded by the town, so it is not possible to admire the ruins in a customary scene of rural isolation. Obviously, the location of the site was not, as recommended, on the fringes of human society; but then the founder of Graiguenamanagh, William the Earl Marshal, was not a man to embrace the ideal of seclusion, and his aims were doubtless strategic rather than entirely religious.

Dunbrody Abbey, Co. Wexford, was founded in the 1170s by Strongbow's uncle, who became its first abbot.

Dunbrody Abbey in County Wexford was the pious work of one Hervey de Montmorency. This uncle of Strongbow was not the sort of benefactor to bask in reflected glory, for he pulled rank to nominate himself the first abbot of the monastery. By all accounts, notably that of Gerald of Wales, this Anglo-Norman baron had not undergone the complete conversion normally required with the taking of the white robe of the Cistercians. 'Would to God that with his monastic garb his mind had become pious and he had laid aside his malicious temper as well as his military habits.' Knowing something of the founder helps us to savour the dour, bulky and embattled aspect of Dunbrody Abbey. Its church 195 feet by 35 feet,

and the 120-feet-square cloister, now visible only as an outline, rank it among the largest of Cistercian houses in Ireland.

Dunbrody, Graiguenamanagh, Tintern, Inch and Grey must be seen not simply as expressions of religious sentiment but as outposts of the conquering power to set alongside the castles of the period. Quite apart from any atonement of personal sin, they signified for the founder a much-valued stronghold, loyal to his own objectives and interests, as well as an instrument of rural development which could stimulate trade in the nearby towns and thereby boost both secular and monastic revenues. But whatever the underlying motives of the founders, Anglo-Norman or Irish, there can be no doubting the tremendous impact of the Cistercians in Ireland. Thirty-three flourishing monasteries in just over a century and a quarter was a remarkable achievement in view of the modest size and resources of the country.

Yet in the cloistered quadrangles behind the walls of stone there was much that did not conform to the overall notion of a Cistercian success story. Links with the mother-abbey in France became weakened by virtue of the long and hazardous journey which made attendance at the annual General Chapter in Cîteaux a duty increasingly to be ignored. Standards declined and politics crept in to the extent that a visitation by Stephen of Lexington on behalf of the order was met with armed resistance at Monasteranenagh and Jerpoint. Mellifont was seething with dissent and lax in its morals. The Abbot of Cîteaux, the headquarters of the Cistercians, complained in a letter to the Pope about conditions in Ireland, lamenting the 'dissipation, dilapidation of property, conspiracies, rebellions and frequent machinations of death'. Nevertheless, order of sorts was reimposed, and the Conspiracy of Mellifont of 1216 was finally suppressed in 1228. Irish idiosyncrasies were ironed out of the system, and Anglo-

Bective Abbey, Co. Meath. The cloister is the loveliest feature; one of its columns has a carving of a cleric.

Norman cultural supremacy set the tone for future recruitment and linguistic practice, or so it was hoped.

The fourteenth century saw a reversal of these reforms, and in line with the Gaelic resurgence Mellifont took the provocative step of making Irish, not French, the language of the statutory oath. The general background was of further devastation caused by the Bruce invasion and widespread fatalities in the course of the Black Death.

The cloister at Jerpoint Abbey was once a sculpture gallery of unparalleled variety. It has been partly restored.

This dreadful pestilence seemed to spare the Irish, striking mainly at the Anglo-Norman towns and not making as much impact in the Gaelic areas of scattered population. One extreme account said that Dublin was entirely depopulated at this time. Given this grim scenario, it is not surprising that there were no new monastic foundations to add to the credit of the Cistercians. In fact the very last was Hore Abbey in County Tipperary in 1272.

There are reports of a further decline of the Cistercian ideal in the fifteenth century as it passed from a philosophy of humble self-sufficiency to one of estate management for profit. Poor financial planning often led to endebtment to foreign bankers. The quest for personal gain impoverished some establishments; and neglect of essential repair caused material decay. Once again occasional fornication produced heirs who inherited an abbacy as their portion. Observance of the rule readily succumbed in the general climate of laxer attitudes and dissolute living. As in the earlier period of moral relapse, there were of course many who remained steadfast and devout. Indeed, the Cistercian movement was far from moribund; and the fifteenth century also witnessed a magnificent surge of rebuilding activity which has bequeathed to Ireland some of her major religious monuments.

The new work at Jerpoint Abbey in County Kilkenny, such as the majestic crossing-tower, represents one of the glories of medieval Ireland. Any vestiges of an adherence to the Cistercian ideal of architectural austerity are swept aside by the cloister at Jerpoint, which in its prime amounted to an eye-dazzling sculptural exhibition. What we encounter today is but a partial reconstruction of the fragments of masonry found scattered about the site. Sadly, many more have gone missing, vanished into the countryside in a manner of speaking. Nevertheless, there is enough here to suggest what an overwhelming experience it must have been to walk through this arcaded cloister.

It is the space between the paired colonnettes which provided the sculptors with a suitably prominent area of stone on which to deploy and display their talents. More than fifty lively carvings have been identified which present us with an enchanting mixture of subjects ranging from clerics and saints to knights and ladies. There is an exuberant showmanship in this courtly parade, doubtless inspired by the benefactors of Jerpoint, the Earls of Ormonde from the mighty Butler family, who had acquired nearby Kilkenny Castle from William the Marshal in 1391. Here we may contemplate the cosy and supportive relationship that existed between noblemen and abbots. A stroll around Jerpoint is rather like intruding on a garden party where the top society people have been suddenly frozen in stone. So lifelike and cheerful are some of the figures that it seems as if the sound of their social banter has only just died on the wind rather than five hundred years ago and more.

Spirited stone carving of a somewhat different nature surfaces at Holycross Abbey in County Tipperary which underwent extensive rebuilding from the 1430s. This was stimulated by donations from the pilgrims come to seek the holy qualities emanating from the much-revered relic of the True Cross. The arms of those Butler Earls of Ormonde, politically astute as ever, appear on the sedilia along with the royal arms of the English monarch. The chancel is rated by some as the best architectural achievement of fifteenth-century Ireland. Holycross Abbey abounds with sculptural delights, superbly carved leaf patterns and animals, of which the most audacious and memorable is the owl on a wall below a corbel. The portrayal is powerful and naturalistic. With wings outstretched, the owl is poised to detach itself from the stonework and take to the air.

Kilcooly Abbey in County Tipperary, the only granddaughter of Mellifont, was reconstructed during the

The splendid tower at Jerpoint was an addition of the fifteenth century over the crossing of the abbey church.

Kilcooly Abbey, Co. Tipperary, possesses some remarkable carvings in relief over the doorway to the sacristy.

second half of the fifteenth century; and the opportunity was taken to use the wall surrounding the new doorway between the north transept and the sacristy as a vast sculptural screen. The work is curiously endearing though crudely executed. The figures of Jesus on the cross and St Christopher fording a stream are ill-proportioned, and the abbot holding a staff and Bible has enormous ears. There is no attempt to align the carvings to the symmetry of the

This abbot with big ears at Kilcooly Abbey was perhaps a deliberate attempt at caricature.

arch; and some details are detached from the composition, such as the alluring mermaid attended by two plump and pleasant-looking fishes. For good measure there are two shields bearing the arms of the Butler family, leaving us in no doubt as to the identity of the patrons. The splendid tomb-chest and effigy of a later scion of that illustrious line, Piers Fitz Oge Butler, carved in the 1520s, reposes in the choir.

Kilcooly, Holycross and Jerpoint form the fourth and final movement of Ireland's Cistercian symphony which had begun in such style with Mellifont. The Anglo-Norman abbeys such as Inch and Dunbrody set up a contrasting second movement. Chaos, reform and conflict were the stuff of a stormy and prolonged third movement. The promise of the uplifting overture was to remain essentially unfulfilled in the finale, which was sculptural and architectural rather than spiritual, so that despite the splendid remains, the Cistercian experience in Ireland may be deemed only a partial success. Though more prominent than the other orders, the Cistercians somehow failed in the long term to enter fully the hearts of the Irish in the manner of the early Celtic monks. That was left to a new breed of reforming monks, the Franciscans, who reinvigorated the monastic ideal and made a distinctly Irish contribution just as the march of history moved inexorably towards the Dissolution.

Kilconnell Friary, Co. Galway, was founded for the Franciscans in 1353 by William O'Kelly, Lord of Hy Many.

A LATE FLURRY OF FRANCISCANS

Rosserk Friary, Co. Mayo. An elegant window frames a fine view out along the west coast of Ireland.

IN THE SOUTH and west of Ireland, usually in remote locations, the eye is caught at intervals by a sight that soon becomes as familiar and as typically Irish as that of the round towers. The graceful, narrow, square tower of Kilconnell Friary in County Galway, watching over a compact group of buildings, is a fine example of the characteristic outline against the sky of a Franciscan establishment in Ireland. There is none of the sprawling splendour of the larger Cistercian houses: the general message of the architecture is one of economy and efficiency. The compactness is largely due to the modest dimension of the cloisters which average around 30 feet square and also to the fact that the usual Franciscan cloister was not a lean-to appendage but an integral part of the structure, carrying an upper storey. Tight intimacy and a sense of enclosure are the distinguishing hallmarks. Once experienced, never forgotten: a Franciscan friary has an atmosphere of its own. It subtly enfolds you in its embrace.

The relatively cramped and gloomy accommodation within is explained by the fact that the 'Grey Friars' spent much of their time out among the people whom they were called to serve. Accordingly, less emphasis was placed on spacious lodgings to while away the passing of the hours. The architectural expression of this basic principle shows the sensible humility of the order and

The magnificent fifteenth-century cloister of Moyne Friary, Co. Mayo, is extremely well preserved and typically Franciscan.

their direct appeal to ordinary folk. Indeed, the friars were themselves drawn from the rank-and-file of the people to whom they ministered. There was no bar to the 'mere Irish' donning the grey habit of the Franciscans. Quite literally, they spoke the same language as the local peasantry.

Elsewhere in the British Isles, the friaries of the Franciscans and of the other mendicant orders were mostly in the towns and cities, and as a result they have succumbed almost completely to the pressures of urban development. Uniquely in Ireland, there remain scattered about the countryside of the west a dozen or so Franciscan houses which, but for their roofs, are remarkably intact; and there are ruined remnants of a further two dozen. Ross Erilly in County Galway is the biggest and best preserved. Rosserk and Moyne, within just a mile of one another in County Mayo, enjoy a marvellous coastal location. Rosserk displays a fine carving of angels on its sedilia as well as a charming miniature portrait in stone of the round tower at nearby Killala. Quin Friary in County Clare was built within the shell of a de Clare castle. What could be more symbolic of Gaelic resistance than this defiant gesture by a Macnamara prince? Muckross Friary in County Kerry has a wonderful cloister which is almost entirely filled by a solitary, ancient yew tree.

The Franciscans first came to Ireland in the early thirteenth century, but most of their foundations were made in the fourteenth and fifteenth centuries when the order was perceived by the Irish as the one closest to their instincts and spiritual needs. By contrast to the Cistercians who reserved their great churches for themselves and the lay brethren, the narrow Franciscan churches were open to the common folk. But although the friars enjoyed the comfort of a well-lit choir in order to read their psalters, the largely illiterate public stood in the relative gloom of the nave, presumably in passive attendance.

The statistics of the Franciscan achievement are telling. During the period 1349 to 1539 not one new abbey in Ireland was founded, but the friaries of the mendicant orders enjoyed an Indian summer with more than a hundred principal and subsidiary houses. Of these the Franciscans supplied the lion's share, as evidenced by the remains of thirty-six friaries, followed by the Dominicans with twenty-nine and the Augustinians with sixteen. These are precious relics of a distinctly Irish heritage.

Muckross Friary, Co. Kerry, where each of the four arcades was constructed in a slightly different manner.

Park's Castle, Co. Leitrim. Where the O'Rorkes of Breffny once lived, a planter built himself a castle.

PLANTATION FEVER

PICTURESQUE Park's Castle on the shore of Lough Gill in County Leitrim has an air of steadfast defence: the five-sided bawn is remarkably high and its corner turrets maintain an apprehensive watch over the lough. Quite possibly, it was a water-borne assault that the English builder of the castle feared might come one day to challenge his possession of the place. After all, Lough Gill had provided the means of escape by boat for the last of the native chiefs of Breffny, one Brian O'Rorke, when cornered in his lair. O'Rorke's desperate flight from the English forces took him as far as Scotland, but he was eventually caught and finally executed in London in 1591. Brian O'Rorke has been described by a twentieth-century bearer of the Breffny name as 'the epitome of a princely Irish leader of the old order'. A ship-wrecked officer from the Spanish Armada, to whom O'Rorke had shown generous hospitality, summed up the qualities of his host in a pithy statement: 'Although this chief is a savage, he is a good Christian and an enemy of the heretics and is always at war with them.'

What happened here, to turn O'Rorke's ancestral stronghold into a planter's castle around the end of the sixteenth century, was no freak of fate or aberration of history but, on the contrary, a symptom of the widespread process known as the Plantations. This was a deliberate, if not always consistent policy of settling English and Scottish Protestants on lands confiscated from rebellious Irish Catholics. However confused the many twists and turns of the various events of the sixteenth and seventeenth centuries may have been, the leitmotif of the period is abundantly clear. The Plantations led to a massive transfer of land ownership; and there occurred, not surprisingly, a sharpening of the conflict between the Irish interests and those of the newcomers. Since Henry VIII had extended the Act of Supremacy to claim leadership of the Irish Church, and then assumed the title of King of Ireland as well, the question of political loyalty could be equated with a simple religious statement. To be a Protestant was to be a trustworthy and loyal subject. To be a Catholic signified an allegiance that was at best dubious.

Ireland at this time was not a rich country, but with huge expanses of land up for grabs the enticement for the mercenary men of Tudor England was to prove irresistible. For those who had missed out on the spoils of the Dissolution of the Monasteries back home, Ireland offered a good chance of making a modest fortune. Perhaps the most successful of the English adventurers of the late Tudor and early Stuart era was Richard Boyle. This once penniless rogue – as he has been described – acquired his vast estates for next to nothing from Sir Walter Ralegh who had been quick to help himself to the opportunities

The stately tomb of Richard Boyle, Earl of Cork, in St Mary's, Youghal, documents the progress achieved by this planter.

of the Munster Plantation from 1586. By all accounts, Richard Boyle demonstrated that it was possible to be a useful and enterprising landlord as well as one with an eye for easy profit. He did much to improve the economic and social conditions of those who lived and worked on his tens of thousands of acres, and was later ennobled as the Earl of Cork. A row of almshouses founded by Richard Boyle still stands in the town of Youghal in County Cork; and in the church of St Mary, Youghal, his imposing tomb commands our attention. This lavish monument in the grandiose style of Jacobean Baroque dominates the south transept which the Earl of Cork had purchased as a private mortuary chapel. For good measure, he had an even more splendid four-tiered extravaganza installed in St Patrick's Cathedral, Dublin. This was the tomb of his wife, Countess Alice Fenton, whose ancestors included a number of officials in the Dublin administration. These characters can be seen as statuettes perched on pedestals on the upper storeys of the monument. Doubtless, this was an elegant political statement of the *arriviste* to claim for himself some form of Irish credentials.

In Ulster, a certain Arthur Chichester did very well for himself and became the Lord Deputy in Ireland of James I, as well as first Baron of Belfast and ancestor of the Marquesses of Donegall. His main claim to lasting fame was as the founder of Belfast. Although the infant city was destroyed by fire in 1708, it was immediately rebuilt and went from strength to strength. But for Arthur Chichester home was Carrickfergus after he had acquired lands there and greatly extended his holdings in Ulster by playing his part in the defeat of the O'Neills. No trace now exists of the palatial residence of Joymount where he lived in great state; but the monumental tomb of the first Baron of Belfast, who died in 1625, may be seen in the church of St Nicholas, Carrickfergus. By contrast to Richard Boyle, who reclines languidly as if relaxing for a moment on the lawn,

Arthur Chichester at rest at Carrickfergus, Co. Antrim, was the landowner who founded the city of Belfast.

the figure of Arthur Chichester is shown in a more devout posture, kneeling in prayer in the company of his wife and infant son.

The dramatic and often violent incidents of the Ulster Plantation are well known. The failed rebellion of Hugh O'Neill, Earl of Tyrone – of which the turning-point was his defeat alongside the Spanish at the Battle of Kinsale in 1601 – led to the departure of the Gaelic leaders into permanent exile in 1607. The 'Flight of the Earls' has been poetically commemorated for all time in the words of the lament: 'Now stolen is the soul from Eire's breast.' What followed was the confiscation of the Ulster lands of the O'Neills which paved the way for the most comprehensive and purposeful of all the Plantations. Within little more than a generation, the resoundingly Gaelic province of Ulster was culturally and politically transformed.

The fate of Hugh Roe O'Donnell, who fought on the losing side at Kinsale and sailed for Spain and an early death, was fairly typical. So too was what happened to his estate in the aftermath of the 'Flight of the Earls'. The fifteenth-century tower-house of the O'Donnells along with their lands in the county of the same name were leased in 1616 to an English army captain, Basil Brooke from Cheshire. Sir Basil – for he was knighted the same year – acquired the lands to hold in permanence in 1623, and he set about extending the tight accommodation of O'Donnell's medieval tower. He built a gabled manor-house in the English style abutting it; and to make the old tower more comfortable and also to create a more balanced architectural composition he likewise adorned it with gables and stately mullioned and transomed windows. Together the two units, a synthesis of fifteenth-century Irish and seventeenth-century English ideas, combined to create a comely residence. Though now roofless, Donegal Castle retains some precious details of the domestic refinements of the period. The truly splendid Jacobean chimney-piece of carved stone with its swags, rosettes, scrolls and escutcheons represents an attempt to reproduce on Irish soil the prevalent fashions of England, and to make this remote Irish property a real home from home. It is one of several such houses in Ireland, of which the first was the Earl of Ormonde's English-style manor at Carrick-on-Suir, seemingly a direct transplant from the Cotswolds with its neat gables and long gallery.

However, a major characteristic of the Ulster Plantation was its strong Scottish flavour. It has been suggested that the dual rule of James I of England as James VI of Scotland had much to do with the encouragement of Scottish settlers. But it can also be observed that the movement of people to and fro between north-east Ireland and south-west Scotland was an old-established pattern of migration and cross-fertilization going back to prehistoric times. It was also the route taken by the Irish colonization of Scotland in the fifth and sixth centuries. Nevertheless, what happened to Ulster in the early seventeenth century was experienced as something akin to a bolt from the blue.

In architectural terms, the Scottish presence has left many tell-tale marks on the Ulster landscape, and none more obvious than Castle Balfour and Monea Castle in County Fermanagh. These stout planters' castles might have been plucked from a Scottish glen where they would be in total harmony with so many others of like style and construction. Monea Castle was the work of the Scot Andrew Hamilton, not a run-of-the-mill planter but a career-minded cleric who rose from his lowly post of Rector of Devenish to become Archbishop of Cashel. The castle was built around 1618–19, adopting a tense defensive posture appropriate to its alien presence in a land that was hardly subdued and quiescent. Indeed, Ulster was to be the flashpoint of an outbreak of spontaneous

Donegal Castle, where Sir Basil Brooke set himself up in baronial style after the Flight of the Earls in 1607.

aggression against the planters which has gone down in history as the Irish Rising of 1641.

This was no military offensive with a well-conceived strategic purpose but an outburst of popular anger and bitterness which spilled over into acts of wanton violence against the Protestant planters and their property. Decades of resentment were suddenly unleashed; and in the chaotic slaughter that followed some two thousand of the settlers were killed. That was bad enough even in an age accustomed to armed conflict, but public opinion in England was possibly more shocked by the reports that many thousands more of the Planters had been stripped of their clothes as well as their possessions and had been driven off like wild beasts to seek refuge where they might.

Monea Castle's precautionary defences had indeed been well advised, but it was none the less not strong enough to withstand the onslaught, and it was one of the victims of the Irish Rising. Sir Toby Caulfield's stronghold of Castle Caulfield in County Tyrone, built at the same time as Monea, had a gatehouse equipped with murder-holes and pistol-loops. But the main house was undefended, and it was taken and burned by the O'Donnellys in the course of the harrowing events of 1641.

The atrocities committed during the Irish Rising were not immediately avenged since England was about to be plunged into almost a decade of the Civil War; but the memory was kept alive and even amplified by propagandists until such time as forces could be committed to Ireland. The fateful moment arrived in 1649 when the victorious Oliver Cromwell was able to despatch 12,000 of his ruthless Ironsides over the Irish Sea. Though he spent but a brief time in Ireland, Cromwell exacted such a terrible retribution that his shadow haunts the country to this day. He left behind a bloody trail of shattered lives and vandalized buildings.

Monea Castle, Co. Fermanagh, was built by a Scot who went on to achieve fame and fortune as the Archbishop of Cashel.

The relaxed and welcoming aspect of Springhill was a sign of more settled times in seventeenth-century Ulster.

In political terms, the outcome of the Cromwellian intervention was a significant tightening of the Anglo-Scottish strangehold on Ireland. The subsequent Restoration of the Stuart Monarchy in 1660 in the person of Charles II brought with it the promise of the return of some estates confiscated from Irish landowners and granted to the Cromwellians, but in the event not much materialized by way of redistribution. The closing decades of the seventeenth century thus saw Irish/Catholic landowners increasingly restricted to the infertile western fringes of the country, while Protestant settlers took control of the better land in the east and the midlands.

The plantation process was rigorously pursued in Ulster, with the laying-out of towns and cities such as Belfast and Londonderry. The more confident mood of the settlers is reflected in a new generation of undefended country houses such as Springhill in County Derry. In addition to the existing old churches used by the Church of Ireland a sprinkling of new Protestant churches arose to serve the spiritual needs of the settler community. There is a fine example in Upper Ballinderry in County Antrim which was completed in 1668. Its pulpit and pews of local oak are laid out in the new auditory fashion, demonstrating how the sermon and lessons had come to replace the mystery of the Holy Sacrament as the determining factor in the planning of churches. Protestantism in Ireland was not, however, just a matter of religious semantics, for it represented an essentially different cultural and social attitude as well. As the official state religion of a new breed of people, it also signified a radically different view of Irish history; and there is possibly no single event capable of such radically opposed interpretation as the defeat of the Catholic forces of the deposed James II of England by the Protestant William of Orange at the Battle of the Boyne in 1690. Together with

The austere and sober mood of Protestant religious architecture is evident in this church at Upper Ballinderry.

the similar outcome at the Battle of Aughrim in the following year the Battle of the Boyne came to symbolize for the Protestant settlers the permanence of their presence in Ireland. To the Catholic natives it was the final nail in the coffin. But, however opposing the viewpoints, the facts were simple enough. The Plantations had taken root.

Kanturk Castle represents a dream unfulfilled for its builder who was ordered to abandon the project.

DREAMS AND DISASTERS

The splendid main door of Kanturk Castle hangs in mid-air like a showroom model of an architectural fixture.

THE CENTURY and a half which elapsed between the direct intervention of Henry VIII as 'King of Ireland' and the defeat of the Irish Catholic cause at the Battle of the Boyne in 1690 was punctuated by many disasters, of which the Cromwellian campaign was but the worst of several horrific visitations. It is a period perhaps best consigned to oblivion, for during it so many Irish dreams turned sour. But before passing on to the more settled, though still far from pacified mood of the eighteenth century, it is of interest to evoke the vicissitudes of those years through the fate of four Irish houses and castles which illustrate some of the nuances of history through the separate destinies of their individual owners.

Dermot MacOwen MacDonogh was an Irish chieftain who attempted to steer a safe course through the treacherous waters of Anglo-Irish politics. Within a few weeks of swearing loyalty and submission to Elizabeth I of England in 1601 he raised a fighting force of 500 men and joined the Spanish side at the Battle of Kinsale. Taken prisoner, he lived to receive a pardon in 1604; and he later regained possession of his lands and resolved to build himself a magnificent castle at Kanturk in County Cork. The extant remains document a fascinating conflation of two essentially different building traditions. It is as if an elegant Elizabethan mansion is struggling to emerge from

Jigginstown House, Co. Kildare, was conceived as Ireland's first grand house in brick with a royal guest in mind.

the rugged, defensive shell of a medieval Irish tower-house. There are some residual pointed arches to remind us of the past, but they are outnumbered by windows of Renaissance modernity; and the delightfully stylish principal entrance is framed by a pair of columns and a round arch. This noble doorway, now stranded at first-floor level without its stairway, shows that the idea of the *piano nobile* may have reached Ireland at this early date. On the other hand, it may well have been the dictates of defence which prompted Dermot to have his front door and main apartments well above the ground.

As it turned out, Kanturk Castle was not to be tested by physical assault. Instead, it was sabotaged by the subterfuge of Dermot's neighbours. It was a mixture of jealousy and apprehension which caused them to denounce the castle – as yet unfinished – as a potential threat to the interests of the English Crown in Ireland. An interdict was promptly placed on the work. The story goes that Dermot, in his fury, smashed all the glass tiles he had bought to make the roof of his dream mansion. A more prosaic version of the tale has it that Dermot's English financiers refused to extend any further what was already a very long line of credit. Whatever the exact circumstances, Kanturk Castle was never to be completed; and its present roofless and floorless state is probably an accurate representation of how it looked in 1615 when the masons downed tools for the last time. There was probably a general feeling of relief in the neighbourhood after this, for stories had been circulating that innocent travellers had been waylaid by Dermot and forced to submit to a regime of slave labour. As for Dermot, he lived to a ripe old age, and he was still spirited enough in 1641 to take his chances and join in the Irish Rising of that year.

Another unfinished fantasy palace, albeit conceived in quite different circumstances, stands broodingly right by the main road from Dublin to Kildare just south-west of

But Jigginstown was never completed; for both the builder, Thomas Wentworth, and his master Charles I were beheaded.

the town of Naas. Jigginstown is the name of this grand manorial house which was the vision of Thomas Wentworth, Earl of Strafford. He was Charles I's Lord Deputy in Ireland, arguably the most efficient administrator and extractor of taxes to have been despatched over the Irish Sea with the commission to find 'the opportunity and means to supply the King's wants'. Wentworth's idea was to create a majestic summer residence, palatial enough to lodge the monarch himself on a future state visit to Ireland. Work began in high hopes. As if to underline the

Burncourt, Co. Tipperary, is a poignant reminder of the bad times endured during the Cromwellian visitation.

novelty and superiority of his scheme, Wentworth opted at Jigginstown to employ the fashionable red brick of Carolean England. So enormous was the project that the bricks – according to an irresistible local legend – were delivered by the hands of a human chain which stretched from the building site all the way to the dockside at Dublin almost twenty miles away.

But like Dermot MacOwen MacDonogh at Kanturk so Thomas Wentworth at Jigginstown was thwarted by the changing whims of fate. A recall to London from his increasingly beleaguered monarch and paymaster Charles I was to lead to the trial and beheading of Wentworth in 1641 as a sacrificial offering to the rising tide of Parliamentarianism that was soon to claim the head of the sovereign himself. And so the grandiose palace of Jigginstown remained uncompleted. The members of the human chain – if they really existed – must have discovered one day that there were no more bricks to be passed on down the line, and presumably they went off in search of some other gainful employment.

What remains of Jigginstown today is not only unfinished but also badly ruined, since the house was stripped of all its lead for ammunition in the 1650s and was subsequently robbed for building materials. The ruins cover a massive 380-feet frontage with a width of 80 feet, supported on a splendidly constructed brick vault for the most part. It was once a building of cathedral-like dimensions. Now the brick walls, reduced to stumps from their original height, stick up at intervals between the empty window spaces like a row of worn and rotten teeth. Somehow there is nothing more desolate than the ruin of a house that was never lived in.

Burncourt in County Tipperary only just escaped falling into that category: its period of occupation was woefully brief. A long-remembered verse tells us that this house was 'seven years in building, seven years living in it and fifteen

The ruins of Burncourt are among the most haunting to be encountered in the Irish countryside.

days it was burning'. The exact figures are questionable, but the essential truth of the matter is conveyed. Burncourt acquired its name following a minor incident during the Cromwellian campaign. It had been built in 1641 by Sir Richard Everard, a Catholic and a Royalist, who had the temerity to inflict military defeat on a force of Parliamen- tarians. One account has it that Cromwell's men burned the place in 1650 in a typical act of revenge; a more heroic version of events is that Lady Everard set the torch to her own home at the approach of the Cromwellian soldiers to deprive them of their pleasure. As for the unfortunate Sir Richard, he was later captured and hanged.

Leamaneh Castle, Co. Clare. From one of these windows 'Red Mary' pushed her hapless husband to his doom.

The impressive ruins of Burncourt show that this was a multi-gabled mansion in the same English tradition as the Ormonde 'castle' at Carrick-on-Suir. Burncourt survives right up to the gables and chimneys, a ghostly, ivy-clad apparition rising up behind the protecting wall of its spacious bawn. it was never rebuilt and has stood defiantly both as a personal memorial to the suffering of the Everards and as yet another reminder of Cromwellian retribution.

One Irish lady who took most unconventional action to

protect the newly built family home from the clutches of Cromwell's invaders was the legendary Máire Ni Mahon, popularly known as Máire Ruadh, 'Red Mary'. This redoubtable woman and her husband Conor O'Brien had just completed a noble extension to their five-storey Irish tower-house of Leamaneh Castle in County Clare, when disaster struck in 1651. Conor O'Brien was killed in the course of an encounter with a detachment of Cromwellian soldiers. When her husband's body was brought home, she defiantly uttered her famous words: 'We need no dead men here.' In fact, Conor O'Brien was not yet dead and his wife nursed him until he expired the following morning. During the night Máire Ruadh found time in the midst of her grieving to think of a way to safeguard the inheritance of her infant son. She promptly set off for Limerick and offered to marry one of the English regiment stationed there in order to avoid the otherwise inevitable dispossession.

Máire Ruadh duly returned home to Leamaneh equipped – as it were – with a certain Cooper as her new consort. What he thought of his Irish wife is not recorded. According to the portrait we have of her she was no classic beauty, and she had a fiery temperament to match her strength of purpose. Her servants went about in fear and dread of her; and she is reputed to have hung some of her inefficient maids by their hair from the corbels of the castle. But she is best remembered for her treatment of her English husband, who was one day foolish enough to let slip a derogatory remark about her former husband Conor O'Brien. The impulsive Máire Ruadh simply pitched him bodily from an upper-storey window of Leamaneh Castle, and he fell to his death. In such peremptory and violent fashion was thereby ended a marriage of convenience which had been born out of the desperate conditions of seventeenth-century Ireland.

The original building at Leamaneh Castle was a tower in the medieval tradition, to which a larger range was added.

Marsh's Library, Dublin. The cause of knowledge was promoted by the public availability of learned books.

DUBLIN REBORN

THE SURGE OF Georgian urbanism which transformed Dublin in the course of the eighteenth century has left us the definitive and enduring image of the Irish capital as one of the great Classical cities of Europe. So radical and far-reaching were the forces unleashed that the Dublin of the Middle Ages was all but obliterated in the process. Even the Castle was subjected to a thorough Georgianization which left but one or two genuine medieval features as tokens of the past. Alone the two cathedrals of Christ Church and St Patrick's stand out, rather like mountain peaks which were high enough to escape the inexorable progress of the rows of brick houses which carried all before them.

Marsh's Library, a neat brick structure built between 1702 and 1707 by Archbishop Narcissus Marsh, provides a convenient vantage point from which to contemplate one chapter of Dublin's evolution from the relative comfort of the one which succeeded it. The library's interior, mercifully unchanged, captures the essence of its period. The planning is orderly, its spirit the quintessence of contemporary modernity offering a storehouse of religious, philosophical and scientific knowledge. This was Ireland's first public library and a flagship of the values of the new age; but it retains some quaint features of the preceding age with its chained volumes and even cage-like contraptions which were designed to lock readers into small compartments so that they could not slip away unsupervised with a volume under their cloak. As if to remind the users of Marsh's Library – 'All Graduates and Gentlemen' – of their privileged position in the vanguard of progress, the elegant sash windows frame a series of magnificent views of St Patrick's Cathedral like a set of old engravings. The agents of rationalism and secularism could thus glance up from their labours and be aware of the dark and mysterious medieval world which was receding daily before their very eyes.

In terms of urban history, the recently restored Tailors Hall, begun in 1706, occupies a similar position to Marsh's Library. As the only surviving guild-hall in Dublin it too provides a bridge of sorts between the eighteenth century and the Middle Ages. Of the sixteenth and seventeenth centuries there remains practically nothing in central Dublin except the church of St Michan which was rebuilt on its ancient site in 1685–6 along with its macabre crypts. These are stuffed with corpses which have been miraculously preserved by the moisture-absorbing properties of the magnesian limestone vaults. Displayed in open coffins, some of these grotesque mummies do open a window on the city's past: you can reach out and touch, as it were, some of Dublin's citizens who walked its fine

The Tailors Hall in Dublin dates back to the beginning of the eighteenth century, when the city was poised for growth.

streets two to three hundred years ago. In many cases organs are visible in outline beneath the leathery skin and the hands retain faint traces of their fingernails. This is a brutal confrontation with history which is not for the faint-hearted.

The really significant monument which spans the gulf between the old world and the new lies further to the west, well beyond the confines of medieval Dublin. The Royal Hospital at Kilmainham was designed by Sir William Robinson, the same who produced Marsh's Library. However, this is no minor architectural essay but a symphony in the grand manner. It was the brain-child of the dazzling Viceroy, the Duke of Ormonde who had followed Charles II into temporary exile and had witnessed at first hand some of the glories of Louis XIV's France. The Royal Hospital at Kilmainham was directly inspired by Les Invalides in Paris; and contrary to what is often believed, its foundation in 1679 preceded that of Wren's Chelsea Hospital in London by three years. Here once again we can see Ireland taking the lead directly from continental Europe.

The 210-foot-square courtyard with its imposing ranges of Classical distinction marks a clear departure from any previous buildings in Ireland. The stately interiors of the central block, comprising the hall, the chapel and the Master's Lodging, leave us in no doubt that the Duke of Ormonde's vision of Dublin, as it emerged into the dawn of the Augustan Age, was not of a provincial outpost but of a national forum, eager to outdo the superior wealth and resources of London. Ormonde's concept of Dublin was to create an Irish version of Paris; and it is to the lasting credit of this inspired Viceroy that the quays along the Liffey were laid out in emulation of those along the Seine. This confident, ambitious mood was to be the sustaining force behind the phenomenal development of the city in the eighteenth century.

The Royal Hospital at Kilmainham, Dublin, inspired by Les Invalides *in Paris and built by the Duke of Ormonde.*

The major symbol of Dublin's idea of itself as the hub of Irish affairs was the Parliament; and it is no coincidence that this was one of the first of the big building projects to be undertaken. Edward Lovett Pearce set to work on his masterpiece in 1729 and created a prestigious home for Irish politics, although the pretensions of the architecture did not escape the acidic wit of the Dean of St Patrick's, Jonathan Swift:

The statue of Burke outside the Neo-Classical façade of Trinity College conveys the intellectual mood of the era.

Tell us what the pile contains?
Many a head that holds no brains.

In fact, Dublin remained subservient to Westminster; but its parliamentarians did at least enjoy vastly superior accommodation since the British Houses of Parliament were not rebuilt until after the fire of 1834. Pearce's building, with later alterations by Gandon and Johnston, still conveys the important role it played not only in the life of the nation but also in the evolving cityscape of Dublin.

Directly opposite the Irish Parliament House – which now serves a rather different purpose as we shall presently see – stood that other bastion of eighteenth-century Dublin, Trinity College. Nothing remains of the original foundation in 1592 of the 'College of the Holy and Undivided Trinity', an Elizabethan institution to educate the sons of Ireland's Protestant community. It was to undergo a complete rebuilding in the course of the eighteenth century to match the intellectual aspirations of the age. The new Trinity College Library of 1712–32 is now the oldest part of the establishment; and it demonstrates the same monumental scale as the Royal Hospital at Kilmainham, declaring quite clearly Dublin's desire to have the biggest and the best. Indeed, it would take the resources of a Renaissance prince to match the staggering 209-foot Long Room of Trinity College Library. Ironically, despite its great size, this building is no longer suitable as a place for students to work in; and it is now used to store and display some 200,000 of Trinity's oldest and most previous volumes, including the Book of Kells.

Even greater things were in store for Trinity College when in 1751 work began to remodel its west front facing the Irish Parliament. The MPs were persuaded to vote a considerable sum towards the project which substantially improved their own view to the east as well as providing

James Gandon's Four Courts exudes a majestic presence on the north bank of the River Liffey in central Dublin.

Dublin with the focal point of a grandiose Classical set-piece. The magnificent Corinthian façade, which has become the visual trademark of Trinity College, arose in the 1750s as the perfect counterbalance to the heroic colonnade of the Parliament House. One of the most striking of vistas, so dear to the spirit of Georgian urbanism, had been positioned in the very heart of Dublin.

Other mighty public buildings were erected with relentless energy. The merchants of Dublin followed the lead given by parliamentarians and academics and commissioned a grandiloquent Royal Exchange in 1769 which, with some alterations, became the City Hall in 1852. Then, amid much controversy and some vocal opposition from the gentlefolk of Dublin, a scheme was drawn up for a new Custom House on the banks of the Liffey. The objections of the leisured classes were clearly stated: 'all Hurry, Crowd and Annoyance which necessarily attend Trade, will be brought even to the Doors of our Nobility and Gentry, and many of those elegant streets in which they now reside, will become the Common Passages for Porters and Cars, loaded with the necessaries of life, and all kinds of merchandise, to be diffused throughout the whole City.' But the commercial dynamism was not to be denied, and the Custom House went ahead. Significantly, the project drew to Dublin the architect who was to make the most powerful individual impact on the city and who brought some touches of grandeur to the nascent metropolis. James Gandon, according to some of the opponents to the Custom House, was 'smuggled into Dublin' in 1781, and he set to work immediately.

Within a few years Dublin had acquired a magnificent riverside building of stature and elegance to supervise and extract the dues from the lively trade which passed over the city's wharves. It was a noble composition as worthy of its prominent waterfront setting as the Doge's Palace in Venice. The picturesque vista across the Liffey has since been marred by a railway bridge in front of the Custom House and some office blocks behind it. The inside was gutted by a fire during the Civil War; and some external details were changed in the subsequent rebuilding. But for all that, it is still a splendid overture on the eastern approaches to Dublin on the banks of the river.

Less than a mile away, also on the north bank of the Liffey, an opportunity presented itself for Gandon in 1786 to design another public building of equivalent weight and significance. This was the Four Courts, a vast complex which is beautifully arranged and orchestrated beneath the watchful presence of its serene lantern-dome. Unlike the Custom House, it retains an uncluttered skyline, against which the statutory on the pediment and balustrade can be properly appreciated. Gandon devoted the rest of his working life to Ireland; and he really dominated the Dublin scene during the last quarter of the eighteenth century.

If Gandon's genius supplied the major public and civic elements in the urban design, then the initiative was well supported by the gentry and aristocracy in a liberal scattering of truly elegant private residences. Leinster House, the town house of the Dukes of Leinster designed in 1745 by Richard Castle, is a model of noble formality. It now accommodates the Irish Parliament: the Dáil Eireann and the Senate. Lord Charlemont, not content with his prestigious mansion which now houses the Municipal Gallery of Modern Art in Parnell Square, put his favourite architect Sir William Chambers to work on a fantastic gem of a second home only a short distance away. The so-called Casino in the Dublin suburb of Marino is quite unlike anything else. This miniature building is more like a Neo-Classical dolls' house or a jewel casket than a serious home, but it none the less contains all the usual domestic features of the day. The need to adapt Mediterranean temple architecture to the vagaries of a Celtic climate resulted in a number of ingenious devices: there are rooftop urns to disguise the chimneypots and drainpipes running inside the hollow stone columns.

Powerscourt House in central Dublin, built in the 1770s for the third Viscount Powerscourt, has survived the vicissitudes of the past two centuries – including use as offices by the Commissioners of Stamp Duties – to

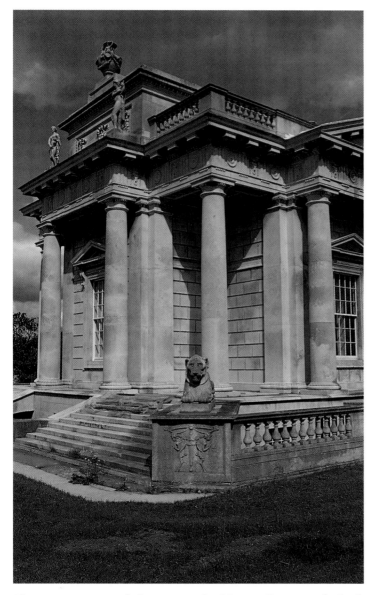

The miniature temple known as the Marino Casino ranks high among the Neo-Classical buildings of its time.

re-emerge in recent years as the centrepiece of an admirably conceived shopping mall. Some of the apartments still display their original plasterwork decoration by Michael Stapleton, a Dublin exponent of the Adam style. Indeed, one of the hidden treasures of Dublin is its scattered collection of the most spirited and finely crafted Rococo plaster to be seen anywhere. Behind some of the solid doors of St Stephen's Green and Lower Dominick Street the walls and ceilings explode in an extravaganza of fanciful stucco. A veritable *tour de force* of the art of the stuccodore awaits in the dome of the Rotunda Chapel, the creation of Robert West. Where there is no space left for angels and cherubs, there are disembodied heads of putti supported on equally disembodied pairs of feathered wings. The dome is all aflutter with life and movement, like an aviary in plaster.

Smart new Georgian churches also came to grace the Dublin scene. Lurking behind a nineteenth-century Romanesque front, St Ann's possesses a glorious interior of 1720s vintage. St Michan's contains some notable Georgian church furniture such as its pulpit, originally on wheels, and the magnificent organ of 1724 said to have been played by Handel when he came to Dublin in the 1740s. On the front of the organ gallery there is an exciting piece of wood-carving, reminiscent of Grinling Gibbons, representing an assemblage of musical instruments which must have delighted Handel. The most significant of Dublin's Georgian churches is St Werburgh's. The interior we see today is that rebuilt in 1759 after a fire gutted the building. This is the quintessence of eighteenth-century Dublin with all attention focused on the ostentatious Royal Coat of Arms adorning the Viceroy's Pew. For St Werburgh's stood right next to the bureaucratic nerve centre and showcase of court ceremonial in Dublin Castle which once safeguarded English interests in Ireland and provided a rallying-point for the

The Georgian doors of Dublin are a hallmark of the city which was a remarkable piece of eighteenth-century urbanism.

Protestant Ascendancy. The Throne Room and St Patrick's Hall convey the period atmosphere of viceregal Dublin at the peak of its fortunes. In the more troubled times that followed, the tower and spire of St Werburgh's, which overlooked the Castle, were perceived as a threat to security; and the offending portions of the church were demolished after a group of eminent architects had been paid to condemn the structure as unsafe.

But the basic stuff of Georgian Dublin which bound together the individual monuments as a cohesive unit was the nexus of streets and squares of uniformly built town houses of bricks and mortar. Unassuming from the outside at first glance, they reveal themselves on closer inspection to be every bit as attuned to the exigencies of elegant display as a parade of cavalry officers. The overall uniformity of appearance actually contains a great variety of stylistic flourishes, notably in the design of the entrance with its characteristic door-hood and fanlight. Subtle differences bear witness to the attempts of the owners to stamp their identity, in however small a way, on their houses. Nowadays many different colours adorn the Georgian doors of Dublin, but absolute conformity within a given street or square was once the norm. The furore which surrounded George Moore's provocative green front door at number 4 Ely Place, when all the other doors were white, led to a virulent feud with his neighbours which only just stopped short of physical violence.

Dublin's Georgian houses have endured a great deal of vandalism and neglect over the years. Mountjoy Square and Henrietta Street, in particular, have come down in the world to a considerable degree. Some of the finest stretches of surviving quality houses are to be found around St Stephen's Green and Merrion Square. St Stephen's Green, extending a quarter of a mile along its sides, is essentially a remnant of Dublin's first green belt established by a late seventeenth-century ordinance that a certain space should be 'wholie kept for the use of citizens and others, to walk & take the open aire'. Merrion Square was Dublin's first planned square in 1762, but the buildings around it were not completed until the beginning of the nineteenth century.

Orderly harmony of the urban machine was provided for in 1757 with the setting up of the 'Commissioners for Making Wide and Convenient Streets'. Known by the shorter title of the 'Wide Streets Commission', this body also established standards for the appearance of the houses which did so much to bring about that conformity

The rusticated façade of this town house in Fitzwilliam Square shows the elegant ambitions of Dublin's builders.

of roofline and fenestration so essential to the Georgian ideal. Some of the streets turned out to be very wide indeed, in complete contrast to the previous narrow lanes and alleys of the old city clustered around the Castle.

Foreign visitors to Dublin in the eighteenth century expressed themselves in very favourable terms about the elegant spaciousness of the Irish capital. Arthur Young, an English traveller of the 1770s, noted that 'the public buildings are magnificent, very many of the streets regularly laid out, and exceedingly well built', but commented

The Bank of Ireland installed itself in the building of the Parliament House designed in 1729 by Edward Lovett Pearce.

too on the parts of the city which had not been subjected to the improvements: 'walking in the streets there, from the narrowness and populousness of the principal thoroughfares, as well as from the dirt and wretchedness of the canaille, is a most uneasy and disgusting exercise.' As the century progressed, developers such as the Gardiner and the FitzWilliam families spread elegance and salubrity before them. The expanding city was home to a population that had boomed from some 60,000 people in 1690 to 130,000 by 1750 and reached as many as 200,000 by the end of the eighteenth century. Against the trend of nearly every other major city in Europe, Dublin's most exclusive and fashionable areas sprouted to the east; and the greatest concentration of deprivation and desperate living conditions was in the south-west.

The north-west sector of Dublin remained untouched by bricks and mortar thanks to the 1752 acres of Phoenix Park which had been set aside by the Duke of Ormonde in the 1660s. This area, five times the size of London's Hyde Park, remained safely beyond the reaches of the Georgian developers and their successors. However, in 1751 the Park Ranger built his official residence in the heart of Phoenix Park; and this was then converted and enlarged in 1815 to serve as the Viceregal Lodge. Despite its colonial style and associations, this is now the seat of the President of Ireland, the Áras an Uachtaráin, a neat and pleasing piece of Regency architecture.

Impressive as it was, the splendour of Georgian Dublin did not lead on to even better things in the nineteenth century. For Dublin, the year 1800 was a watershed, for that was when the Irish Parliament voted itself out of existence in approving the Union with Britain. Ironically, some of the very people who had helped make Dublin a metropolis of international repute now perceived their own interests to lie in the Union, which turned Dublin

Henry Grattan's statue outside the erstwhile Parliament House is a reminder of the building's original purpose.

into a provincial outpost of an administration based in Westminster. There were economic repercussions to the demise of the Irish Parliament. We hear that Lord Cloncurry paid £8000 for the lease of his house at 24 Merrion Square, but could obtain only £2500 for it ten years later – after the Union.

Not that the physical aspect of Dublin suddenly changed as a result of Ireland's new political status; but something of the heart and soul of the city departed along with its Members of Parliament and those who lobbied them. Huge buildings such as the ill-fated General Post Office of 1815 continued to go up, but they no longer reflected the underlying mood of Dublin. As for the Irish Parliament House, brave symbol of seventy years of heated debate, it was totally redundant. The British government lost no time in selling it to the Bank of Ireland; and a covenant was included in the deeds of the sale that both chambers should be completely altered. Furthermore, it was seen to that external modifications should 'reconcile the citizens' to the changed circumstances. By good fortune, the chamber of the House of Lords survived, and the outside work was sensitively handled. So the Irish Parliament still stands, though it now accommodates commercial bankers. But the statue of Henry Grattan in the street adjacent to the noble colonnade adds a wry comment of its own. This dramatic portrayal of perhaps the most forceful of Ireland's eighteenth-century parliamentarians appears to be continuing the interrupted debate with arm outstretched as if in protest at the infamy of it all.

Castletown House, Co. Kildare. A flanking pavilion and elegant colonnade hint at the magnificence of this Palladian house.

HOUSES OF THE ASCENDANCY – THE CLASSICAL AGE

THE TREATY OF LIMERICK of 1691 which concluded the hostilities, for the time being at least, between Protestant and Catholic, could have been a force for eventual reconciliation had its provisions for the status of Catholics been respected. Instead, the Protestant magnates succeeded in introducing a whole series of measures designed to marginalize Catholics in every practical sense. The Penal Laws, as they are collectively known, ranged from barring Catholics from buying or inheriting property, excluding them from public office and parliamentary representation, to curbs on education and religious worship. There was even a petty rule that no Catholic could own a horse worth more than £5. Although some of the Penal Laws were clearly impossible to enforce, those concerning land ownership did have a radical effect; and historians have produced some startling statistics to illustrate the point. By around 1700 Ireland's Protestants, representing at most 20 per cent of the population, owned over 90 per cent of the land.

Being Protestant, however, did not mean an automatic allegiance to England. Indeed, it was quite the opposite with many of the greatest of Irish patriots from Henry Grattan and Wolf Tone to Charles Parnell who all belonged to the Protestant community. There was a solid Irish core in the consciousness of the Protestant Ascendancy – as the landowning class was called – which makes the reading of eighteenth- and nineteenth-century Irish history particularly awkward for those who prefer a simple black-and-white scenario. Could there be a more equivocal phenomenon than a later son of the Protestant Ascendancy, William Butler Yeats, espousing the Celtic Revival of ancient Irish culture as well as sticking up proudly for the contribution made to Ireland by those of his own creed and background? 'We are no petty people. We are one of the great stocks of Europe. We are the people of Grattan; we are the people of Swift, the people of Emmet, the people of Parnell. We have created the most of the modern literature of this country. We have created the best of its political intelligence.' In this extraordinary outburst of sectarian pride Yeats might also have added country houses and landscaped parks to the list of the Ascendancy heritage; for these are the major physical achievements through which we can still enter the privileged world of eighteenth-century Ireland and sample its peculiar charms.

The Ascendancy was evidently not an aristocratic closed shop. Castletown House in County Kildare, the first and the most splendid of the big houses, was built by a certain William Conolly, son of an innkeeper in County Donegal. Speaker Conolly, as he is popularly known from his office in the Irish Parliament, amassed a fortune through a series of astute dealings in forfeited estates in the post-1690s era when vast swathes of the country changed hands. His house is a gigantic affair, quite beyond what had been seen before in Ireland. Its massive Palladian frontage towers monumentally above the meadows that border the River Liffey. Even before you enter Castletown House the ambition of its creator communicates itself. This was an act of bravado from the man reputed to be the richest in Ireland at the time. Quite simply, he wanted the best that money could buy. Accordingly, the house façade was not in any way provincial or undiscriminating in taste but a grand Palladian production from the drawing-board of Alessandro Galilei who had previously designed the front elevation of St John Lateran in Rome. The construction of Castletown, commenced in 1722, was later supervised by Edward Lovett Pearce, the architect of the Irish Parliament. It was Pearce who added those scenically curved colonnades which connect the main block to two charming pavilions.

This stylistic flourish was not art for art's sake, though the device does enhance the overall composition, but an artful disguise for those utilitarian features of a grand establishment, the stables and the kitchen. In this, Pearce did much to promote one of the most important elements of Andrea Palladio's Italian villas which were essentially working farms presented as Classical houses, a successful formula that was to prove equally popular in an Irish context. Many houses, both great and small, in Ireland greet the visitor with a similarly disposed pair of colonnades as if with open arms.

Hospitality was ever a matter of the utmost importance in the noble houses of Ireland; and Speaker Conolly was not one to turn away a stranger on his doorstep. One day this had unfortunate consequences, for there is a story that the devil disguised in human clothes managed to get himself asked in for supper at Castletown. Speaker Conolly discovered this when he bent down to retrieve a napkin and saw that his companion had removed his boots to reveal hairy ankles and cloven hooves. He called

a priest to exorcize his unwelcome guest. A breviary was hurled which cracked the mirror, whereupon the devil leapt on to the hearthstone and cracked it before disappearing up the chimney in a cloud of smoke. Both mirror and hearthstone bear the signs of the diabolical visitation.

But the overall atmosphere of Castletown is of a house designed expressly for the parade of pleasure: parlour games and refined pursuits for the ladies, hard drinking by red-faced squires and parliamentarians. Speaker Conolly did not live long enough to see it all completed, dying childless in 1729, and there was a period of limbo before the final touches were added by his grand-nephew Thomas Conolly and his artistic wife Louisa Lennox, daughter of the Duke of Richmond. Soon after their marriage in 1758 Thomas and Louisa engaged the famous Francinis to apply their skills in stucco decoration to the imposing stairwell at Castletown.

The prodigious career of the Francinis as the masters of fanciful plasterwork in Ireland came about by chance, for they were on their way to America when they became shipwrecked off the Irish coast. With the enormous boom in country house building about to take off, they found more than enough outlets for their superlative talents. America's loss was Ireland's gain. The Francinis were also much in evidence at Russborough in County Wicklow, another Palladian masterpiece, designed by Richard Castle. The sumptuous house employs the same curving colonnades as seen at Castletown, here used to create an even more triumphal effect along a 700-feet frontage. The builder of Russborough was also of modest origins: Mr Joseph Leeson inherited a fortune in 1740 from his father, a prosperous Dublin brewer. His subsequent elevation as the Earl of Milltown matched in every respect the majestic state of his country house of Russborough.

But to return to Castletown for a moment, let us briefly enter the Long Gallery, now bare of furniture and reveal-

Russborough, Co. Wicklow. A noble staircase and a regal lion extend a formal welcome to this great mansion.

ing the vastness of its conception, and try to imagine the grand effect it once made as described by a visitor, Lady Caroline Dawson, in 1778:

> We then went to the house, which is the largest I ever was in, and reckoned the finest in this kingdom. It has

been done up entirely by Lady Louisa, and with a very good taste. But what struck me most was a gallery, I daresay 150 feet long, furnished in the most delightful manner with fine glasses, books, musical instruments, billiard table – in short, everything you can think of is in that room; and though so large, is so well fitted, that it is the warmest, most comfortable-looking place I ever saw. They tell me they live in it quite in the winter, for the servants can bring dinner or supper at one end without anybody hearing it at the other; in short I never saw anything so delightful.

So let us slip away quietly and leave Louisa and her companions engaged in their decorative schemes to further beautify the magic realm, and visit another Palladian house of more modest proportions. Strokestown Park in County Roscommon was designed by Richard Castle, though much of his work was subsequently modified. Unlike Castletown, Strokestown was conceived primarily as a working farmhouse, albeit of an elaborate kind. Here again, the stable and the kitchen have been gracefully transformed into elegant pavilions linked to the main house. The stable building is of particular note; a glorious series of vaults supported on a central line of Tuscan columns fully justify their description as an 'equine cathedral'. Fascinating too is the galleried kitchen, which permitted the lady of the house to drop the menus for the week, as if from the bridge of a ship down into the engine room, where the staff toiled over the hot stoves. A final contrivance should be noted: a gloomy brick tunnel runs beneath the house, connecting stable-yard and kitchen-yard, so that the servants could pass dry-shod and unseen from one to the other. Altogether, Strokestown Park evokes so much of the day-to-day life of an eighteenth-century country house in Ireland. Even the furniture tells a story. On the one hand, there is a semicircular claret table especially designed for bouts of drinking which contained a net for catching the empty bottles as they were tossed aside one by one. But books were not despised at Strokestown, for they were accommodated in a monumental Chippendale bookcase of prestigious craftsmanship.

Strokestown Park House, Co. Roscommon, where the stable by Richard Castle is a highly acclaimed feature.

The Palladian formula flourished virtually unchallenged in Ireland for about fifty years, and it was often applied to existing houses such as Florence Court in County Fermanagh which received its pavilions linked to the central block by balustraded arcades in the 1770s. However, by this time fashions were slowly changing and inspiration was being sought no longer exclusively in the Renaissance style of Andrea Palladio but also in the Neo-Classical imitation of the original buildings of the Greeks and Romans. At the same time, a taste for frivolous exotic features was manifesting itself in everything from medievalisms to orientalisms. A man to cater for all tastes of the Irish gentry was the Englishman James Wyatt, who managed to complete an impressive body of work in Ireland, though with only one recorded visit to the country. Westport House in County Mayo was transformed in the 1780s by some opulent Wyatt interiors in the Neo-Classical style, of which the dining-room is the main survivor. One of the upstairs rooms has retained its original Chinese wallpaper which is reputed to have been acquired by Wyatt himself. Westport House was the home of that Regency buck *par excellence* the second Marquess of Sligo who travelled for a while with Byron in Greece and was one of the early 'excavators' who plundered archaeological sites such as Mycenae for portable antiquities. On a voyage back from the Mediterranean he bribed some sailors of His Majesty's Navy to help him navigate his way home. For this he was fined £5000 and sent to Newgate gaol for four months. His widowed mother ended up falling in love with the judge and marrying him when her wayward son had served his sentence. Ascendancy life so often resembled a comic opera played by larger-than-life characters.

Westport illustrates yet another colourful strand in the complex yarn of Irish history for the house is built on the site of an earlier building which replaced the tower of the

Westport House, Co. Mayo. The vogue for Chinese wallpaper reached as far west as the Atlantic coast of Ireland.

Every aspect of Castle Coole, Co. Fermanagh, reflects the pure vision of this Neo-Classical country house.

legendary Grace O'Malley, the warrior queen and buccaneer who earned the respect of Elizabeth I of England as a woman after her own heart. The dungeons of Grace O'Malley's castle lurk beneath Westport as a symbol of the ancient womb from which the present noble residence is sprung; and the blood of that indomitable woman eventually flowed into the line from which the present Marquess of Sligo is descended.

James Wyatt, whom we encountered at Westport as a talented decorator, reveals himself at another Irish house to be an architect of quite exceptional vision. Castle Coole in County Fermanagh is arguably the purest realization in Ireland of the Neo-Classical ideal. This Hellenic creation is so austerely conceived and finely honed that it takes the breath away. Built between 1790 and 1797 for Lord Belmore, the house expresses perfectly the mood of Grecian simplicity which appealed to those with a serious interest in antiquity. This is a world removed from the frivolities of the age such as the vogue for Rococo plasterwork, or the guileless domesticity of the 'cottage orné' such as may be seen at Derrymore House in County Armagh. Castle Coole exudes stylistic purity in every detail, so that one can easily imagine the architect as a man obsessed with the Grecian spirit. Yet James Wyatt could turn his hand just as well to Gothic, as may be witnessed to stunning effect by Slane Castle in County Meath, where the ballroom has been hailed as the most spectacular early Gothic Revival interior in Ireland.

There is a further dimension to the unreality of Castle Coole when we learn that James Wyatt never came to see his masterpiece. It was also spurned by George IV on his visit to Ireland. The State Bedroom was prepared expressly for the royal visit, but George IV preferred to spin out his stay at Slane Castle in amorous dalliance with Lady Conyngham. Perhaps the most telling comment on the perfection of Castle Coole was the enigmatic remark

An exotic garden serves as an overture to the house at Mount Stewart, Co. Down, built in the eighteenth and nineteenth centuries.

by a contemporary French visitor that it was better 'to leave the Temples to the Gods'. This could imply either a general disapproval of Neo-Classical ideology or a veiled compliment that it had come too close to its ideal for comfort. Ambivalence is perhaps the underlying message of Castle Coole, for it poses the unanswerable question about the ultimate merit of the direct transplantation of form from one culture to another. To add to the uncertainty about where it really belongs, it can be said that the main aspect about it that is truly Irish is the setting. The design, the Portland stone, and some of the masons and master craftsmen responsible for the scagliola and

The passion for ancient Greece inspired the Temple of the Winds at Mount Stewart. It was built by James Stuart.

plasterwork were all imported – at enormous expense – from England, where Wyatt masterminded the entire project inside and out by remote control thanks to excellent communication with the supervisor on the spot. Castle Coole is thus a remarkable achievement in organizational terms as well as an aesthetic experience to be savoured.

James Wyatt was also commissioned to produce drawings for the remodelling of Mount Stewart in County Down for the Marquess of Londonderry, but the plans were never executed. The Neo-Classical rebuilding awaited the arrival of George Dance in 1804–5, and, more importantly, that of William Vitruvius Morrison in the 1830s. The hall, a huge octagon entered through pairs of Ionic columns painted to simulate the effect of green marble, is as serious a study in Greek Revival as Castle Coole. This space was probably intended to serve as a sculpture court; and it contains two nineteenth-century copies of Classical nudes as well as a Greek pentelic marble tombstone dating from around 350 BC. However, Greek enthusiams had already manifested themselves at Mount Stewart in the 1780s when an entrancing 'Temple of the Winds' had been built in the grounds to the design of James 'Athenian' Stuart.

Located about half a mile away from the main house, Mount Stewart's 'Temple of the Winds' is an accurate copy of the Athenian original but for the balconies over the porticos. After all, the building was designed to be no slavish imitation done for academic satisfaction but to be used as a delightful banqueting house away from it all on a knoll enjoying panoramic views over Strangford Lough. The third Marquess of Londonderry, when confronted with a proposition to turn it into a mausoleum, responded tartly: 'I have no Taste for Turning a Temple built for Mirth & Jollity into a Sepulchre. The place is solely appropriate for a Junketing Retreat in the Grounds.' It was

Mussenden Temple at Downhill was a clifftop library created for one of Ireland's most eccentric aristocrats.

also, of course, a seductive eye-catcher in a picturesque landscape.

No gentleman with a taste for ancient Greece or Rome could be without such a Neo-Classical embellishment in his park; and Frederick Hervey, Earl of Bristol and Bishop of Derry, was not a man to forgo anything at all which offered him pleasure. The Earl Bishop collected paintings, statues and women with an unrelenting passion that was fuelled by an enormous fortune. In the grounds of his Neo-Classical mansion of Downhill in County Derry he erected an exquisite rotunda, ostensibly as a library, but perhaps also for occasional junketing. Though now devoid

Castle Ward, Co. Down, where the Gothic whims of a wilful lady have left a permanent mark on a country house.

of books and any internal decoration, Mussenden Temple – for he dedicated it to a female cousin of that name – remains a magnificent sight, perched on the very edge of a cliff and commanding extensive views along the coast. Equally magnificent were Frederick Hervey's exploits in Ireland, England and Italy, which have a Byronic grandeur to them. Like the poet he also died abroad in miserable circumstances. A sudden attack of gout laid him low just outside Rome; and he breathed his last in a rustic outhouse because the peasant farmer did not want to have a Protestant priest dying under his Catholic roof. It would have been a fitting retribution for many a member of the Protestant Ascendancy, but the Earl Bishop may have reflected ruefully on the injustices of the world, for he had earned himself a reputation for religious tolerance by allowing Catholic Mass to be celebrated in the room beneath his Mussenden Temple.

The Neo-Classical fashion was not unanimously followed in Ireland. The Gothic treatment of Birr Castle in County Offaly as well as Slane Castle in County Meath was a sign of things to come in the nineteenth century. And most remarkably of all at Castle Ward in County Down, a veritable 'Battle of the Styles' was waged within the context of a single house. The rebuilding of Castle Ward should have been, according to the master of the house Bernard Ward, later elevated to the peerage as Lord Bangor, another resplendent jewel in the Palladian crown. But he had reckoned without the architectural wishes of his wife, Lady Anne. One can only imagine the domestic scene as the Wards fought it out over the conflicting styles of Classical and Gothic. A visitor to the place in 1762 summed it up rather pointedly: 'He wants taste and Lady Anne Ward, his wife, is so whimsical that I doubt her judgement. If they do not do too much they can't spoil the place, for it hath every advantage from nature that can be desired.' What role the architect played in all this is unknown, for he conspired to remain anonymous; but what he produced at the end of the day was Ireland's most famous architectural compromise. Lord Bangor's half of the house was of conventional Palladian cut, and Lady Bangor's a sort of Strawberry Hill Gothic, although as one can judge from the regular fenestration, the lay-out of the house inside was thoroughly Classical. The dichotomy of taste was also reflected in the interior decoration. One passes from the stately, male, Graeco-Roman domain of the hall and the library to the female realm of the saloon,

Fota House, Co. Cork, shows that the Neo-Classical style was still much in favour in the early nineteenth century.

The vestibule of Fota House – though not on the grand scale – is the epitome of well proportioned elegance.

the morning room and above all the Gothic Boudoir, where Lady Bangor's medievalist whimsy is most apparent. The ceiling bulges in plaster imitation of the fan-vaulting of the Henry VII Chapel at Westminster, but the effect is rather ponderous and unlovely. John Betjeman described the impression he had of it as like 'standing under the udders of a cow'.

After the separation of the house into its stylistic halves followed the separation of the marriage. Lady Bangor retired to Bath, where she died in 1798. It might have been some consolation for her to know that Gothic was, in the more serious mood of the Gothic Revival, to sweep all before it by the middle of the nineteenth century. But she was ahead of her time; and Neo-Classical remained the dominant mode in Ireland during the early years of the new century with such fine productions as Lissadell in County Sligo, Fota House in County Cork and Emo Court in County Laois. There was apparently some doubt in the mind of John Smith-Barry at Fota, to whom William Vitruvius Morrison submitted both a Neo-Classical as well as a Tudor design for the rebuild in the 1820s. The tide was already turning in favour of Gothic but the master of Fota opted for the tried and trusted Neo-Classical option which we see today, orchestrated to such stunning effect.

However, stylistic correctness was not generally of paramount importance, and some of the more endearing Irish houses of the period are those in which there has been no attempt to make an architectural statement of belief. Bantry House in County Cork is a curious amalgam of several currents of the eighteenth and nineteenth centuries. It was built in 1771, probably around an earlier house, but it was much later that it acquired its present external aspect with brick pilasters topped by Corinthian capitals on the rear elevation. The entrance to the house is guarded by larger-than-life models of herons with crowns around their necks. These three-dimensional embodiments of the coat of arms of the Earls of Bantry look out on a palatial garden dotted with urns and statues. Some of the interiors are in the French manner of the *grand siècle*, and the house is crammed with the most exquisite items purchased at bargain prices from the bankrupt French aristocracy during the lean years that followed the Revolution. The Rose Drawing-room is the delicate quintessence of pre-Revolution France, but the dining-room is a full-blooded Baroque concoction in which the twin portraits of George III and Queen Charlotte survey the scene from the

Bantry House, Co. Cork, where the dining-room is observed by proud portraits of George III and Queen Charlotte.

The gardens of Bantry House climb a steep hill which permits this view over the rooftop towards Bantry Bay.

splendour of their gilt frames of the most elaborate Rococo imaginable.

Bantry House, for all its charm and nonchalance, drags us back into the troubled waters of Irish politics, for the scene it commands is Bantry Bay where in 1796 a French fleet dropped anchor in an invasion attempt organized by Wolfe Tone, a leader of the Society of United Irishmen. This was the inauspicious prelude to the ill-fated rising of 1798 and another failed French invasion which led to the capture and death of the idealistic Wolfe Tone. It was the growing stridency of the cries for Irish independence which prompted the authorities in London to push through the Irish Parliament what it was hoped would be the final solution, namely the total fusion of government of Ireland and Britain. The Act of Union received royal assent on 1 August 1800, having been approved in the Irish Parliament by 138 votes to 96. It came into force on 1 January 1801. Henceforth Ireland was incorporated as an integral part of the United Kingdom.

The Union, though essentially achieved through the votes of the Protestant Ascendancy, was a question on which many of its members had a divided loyalty. Class allegiance and personal interest were often in conflict with cultural sympathies and an individual's sense of an Irish identity. But the day of reckoning had been postponed, at least for the time being, as the front line of Irish politics was transferred from Dublin to London, where 100 Irish MPs represented the aspirations of the country at Westminster. For a while the tumult in Ireland subsided, and the merry social whirligig was resumed in the big country houses up and down the land. Links with England inevitably strengthened, and the hand of English architects made an ever stronger impact on the changing face of Ireland.

The Ascendancy houses of the eighteenth century were thus born of and into a very different social climate from their nineteenth-century successors. They possessed an exuberance of spirit that was splendidly evoked by the Palladian and Neo-Classical architecture, conjuring up sun-lit Mediterranean visions which defied the often gloomy Nordic climate. This was a world, for all the unfairness on which its rank and fortunes were based, which had a real eye for beauty, refinement and enjoyment. There was a tangible zest for life which, as the nineteenth century unfolded, went flat and degenerated into a more forced gaiety in the *fin de siècle* quest for physical pleasure and material success in the face of changing political realities.

Given the democratic and egalitarian climate of our times, it is impossible to exclude a note of censure from our evaluation of the houses of the Ascendancy, for they were the bastions of privilege in their day. But for all that, many of the Ascendancy families were a positive economic and social force in their localities with their estate improvements, housing schemes and even projects of urbanistic ambition. Ireland's provincial towns and villages owe more than those of almost any other European country to the efforts of local landowners, who acted not altogether altruistically but out of enlightened self-interest. Places as diverse as Westport in County Mayo, Strokestown in County Roscommon and Birr in County Offaly represent some of the most impressive examples of landlord planning.

As for the grand houses themselves, many have fallen victim to the radically changed financial circumstances of their owners or to the hazards of fire and other calamities. The palatial central block of Powerscourt in County Wicklow, once a proud and richly furnished Palladian mansion of 1730s vintage, survived all dangers over almost two and a half centuries only to be gutted by a violent conflagration in 1974, a year before it was due to open to the public. However, the gardens may be visited; and it is still a thrilling experience to stand on the baronial terraces and to contemplate, along with the distant view of the Wicklow Hills, the dreams and visions of generations past. Although many of the Classical houses of the Ascendancy have succumbed to the ravages of time, enough remain to conjure up a beguiling image of that remote world of convivial refinement. The Irish Georgian Society fights on with courage and limited resources to safeguard what is left, and has notched up some remarkable successes such as the acquisition of Castletown House, with which Speaker Conolly launched that grand enthusiasm for the stately homes of Ireland.

A traditional Irish cabin at Rosmuck, Co. Galway, expresses the primitive but picturesque lifestyle of the countryside.

LIFE ON THE LAND

BETWEEN THE world of the great country houses and that of the common folk there extended a huge and unbridgeable gulf. Constance Markievicz (*née* Gore-Booth) gives us a rare insight into the rural conditions of late nineteenth-century Ireland, as observed from one of the country's noble drawing-rooms in Lissadell in County Sligo:

> You saw the landlords in their big demesnes, mostly of Norman or Saxon stock, walled in and aloof, an alien class, sprung from an alien race ... The prosperous farmers were mostly Protestant ... and hidden away among rocks in the mountain sides or soaking in the slime and ooze of the boglands or beside the Atlantic shore where the grass is blasted yellow by the salt wind you find the dispossessed people of the old Gaelic race in their miserable cabins.

'Dispossessed' is the key word to describe the status of the Irish countryfolk. Some of the native chieftains had been made the owners of enormous estates through the Tudor policy of 'surrender and regrant', whereby territories that had been held by the community of the tribe were suddenly vested in individuals. But the owners of the land were mostly the descendants of the settlers and colonizers who had come to Ireland in a steady flow since the days of Strongbow. The various confiscations had inexorably whittled away the number of estates in Irish hands to a marginal few; but the rank-and-file of the rural population had not followed their leaders into exile. They stayed put, obdurate and as unwilling to move as barnacles on a ship's hull, even though they were obliged to rent their lands from people who were not of their kind.

As for the 'miserable cabins' in which the 'dispossessed' lived, they had been the object of much comment both from travellers and bureaucrats. According to the 1841 Census some 40 per cent of all houses in Ireland were of the lowest category, mud-cabins of only one room. In the poorer and overpopulated west the proportion was probably nearer 75 per cent. Numerous accounts survive of the primitive conditions, such as the following early nineteenth-century description of a cabin in Clifden in County Galway:

> There was only a kitchen and one room. In the kitchen were a cow, a calf, a dog, three or four hens and a cock fluttering noisily about, and in a corner a coop full of chickens. Here I slept on the ground near the ashes of a glowing peat fire; and in the other room slept the family – the father and mother, two girls and a boy. The silence of the night was broken from time to time by the thud and splash of dung on the mud floor, and the crowing and clatter of the fowls woke me early.

Unhygienic as it sounds, such a quantity of livestock and two rooms actually indicate a relatively well-off family by the standards of the day. The least fortunate folk squatted in ditches or in roadside hovels like 'bird's nests, of dirt wrought together and a few sticks and some straw, and like them are generally removed once a year'. Even those familiar with the Irish scene, such as Michael Dohenny – one of the Young Irelanders of 1848 – were shocked by a cabin near Killarney where 'the dung of the cattle had not been removed for days, and half-naked children squatted in it as joyously as if they rolled on richest carpets'.

Those observers not completely repelled by the physical squalor often had a sympathetic eye for the human qualities of the cottier class, as they were collectively called by the social historians. Sir Walter Scott in 1825 on his Irish journey encountered 'perpetual kindness in the Irish cabin; buttermilk, potatoes, a stool is offered, or a stone rolled that your honour may sit down . . . and those that beg everywhere else seem desirous to exercise hospitality in their own houses'. Even a bureaucrat of the Census Commissioners thought it worth recording 'the proverbial gaiety and lightheartedness of the peasant people'. Scott also noted that 'their natural condition is turned towards gaiety and happiness'. And in many contemporary accounts we read of the tremendous importance attached to dancing, music, singing and story-telling.

Exceptionally we also encounter a composer of verses among the cottiers, one Andrew McKenzie on the Ards Peninsula in County Down. His name suggests a Scottish origin, but his wry and revealing commentary shows that he was no stranger to the conditions experienced by millions in rural Ireland in the early nineteenth century:

. . . I never learn'd a trade
But daily wield a flail or spade.
Endeav'ring to preserve in life,
Six naked children and a wife.
My mansion is a clay-built cot,
My whole domain a garden plot –
For these, each annual first of May
Full thirty shillings I must pay:
Ye who in stately homes reside,
Th'abodes of luxury and pride,
May deem it false when I assert,
My house would scarcely load a cart;
So little straw defends its roof,
Against the rain it is not proof.

The poet then supplies an inventory in verse of the paltry items with which his 'cot' is furnished, and he concludes with details of the family menu:

One moment yet I beg you'll spare,
And just look o'er my bill of fare,
Which with my furniture accords,
And small variety affords;
The cruel butcher's murd'rous knife
For me deprives no beast of life;
No angler with ensnaring wiles,
For me the finny race beguiles:
No sailor braves the dangerous sea
To bring home luxuries for me –
But words I will not multiply,
Potatoes all our meals supply;
A little milk to them we add –
And salt, when that can not be had.

The humble potato, ironically celebrated here as the staple food of the McKenzie family, should not be lightly dismissed as a domestic detail; for the unassuming tuber was to play a role in the unfolding drama of rural Ireland that can hardly be exaggerated. Since the time of its introduction into Ireland in the late sixteenth century by Tudor colonists – and Sir Walter Ralegh is usually credited with the momentous deed – the potato rapidly established itself as the ideal food for Irish conditions by virtue of its high nutritional value and ease of cultivation. It has been calculated that just one acre of land sufficed to feed a family of five to six people for most of the year. A simple spade was all that was required to cultivate the 'lazy beds' of earth in which the potatoes grew. With the trend towards subdivision of the land into ever smaller plots which yielded the maximum return to the landlord, there was much merit in a food crop that could be extracted with relative ease and could sustain vast numbers of people on smallholdings. Indeed, it has been argued that the potato made it all possible; both for the Irish population of 4 million in 1781 to more than double by 1841, and for holdings to become increasingly minute. By the 1840s some 64 per cent of the holdings in Connacht were smaller than 5 acres. Nationwide, the potato constituted the sole source of food for about 3 million people.

There had been various warnings that this was a precarious and potentially dangerous dependence on one crop, for there occurred sporadic failures of the potato harvest. Then, between 1845 and 1848 the potato blight known as *Phytophthora infestans* struck hard and repeatedly, causing the most awful famine which visited upon the country areas unimaginable hardship and suffering. Crops that looked healthy when dug up rapidly went mouldy and disintegrated into a foul-smelling putresence. Thus the entire food supply of millions of people vanished before their eyes. Diseases such as typhus, dysentery, famine dropsy and even cholera followed hard on the heels of starvation. And to cap it all, the winter of

The canal at Cong, Co. Mayo, was one of various public works intended to relieve the suffering of the poor.

1846–7 was one of the most bitterly cold that Ireland had ever experienced.

The statistics tell a harrowing tale. Of the 1841 population of 8,175,124 there remained in 1851 only 6,552,385. Without the famine the population should have been expected to rise in excess of 9 million, so that as many as 2.5 million people had disappeared from the face of the land. Death and emigration accounted for the loss in roughly equal measure. But what the naked statistics, shocking as they are, cannot convey is the reality of the intense physical pain of it all. A report from Skibbereen in County Cork recorded in December 1846:

I entered some of the hovels ... and the scenes that presented themselves were such as no tongue or pen can convey the slightest idea of. In the first, six famished and ghastly skeletons, to all appearance dead,

Flax was the raw material behind the relative rural wealth of the linen weavers. (Ulster-American Folk Museum.)

were huddled in a corner on some filthy straw, their sole covering what seemed a ragged horse-cloth, and their wretched legs hanging about, naked above the knees. I approached in horror, and found by a low moaning they were alive, they were in fever – four children, a woman and what had once been a man.

Other heart-rending accounts tell of people too weak to bury their dead, seeing the bodies of their loved ones devoured by dogs and rats.

Humanitarian aid initiated by the Prime Minister Sir Robert Peel was countermanded by his successor Lord John Russell; and much was then left to the voluntary agencies and to programmes of public works to distribute relief. These required the starving and the destitute to labour on a number of projects, mainly conceived by insensitive and incompetent bureaucrats. One official admitted that 'Roads were laid out which led from nowhere to nowhere; canals were dug into which no drop of water has ever flowed; piers were constructed which the Atlantic storms at once began to wash away'. One such scheme may be seen near Cong in County Mayo, where the idea had been to connect Lough Corrib and Lough Mask by a navigable canal cut through the limestone terrain. Unfortunately, the porous nature of the rock thwarted all attempts to fill the canal, for the water simply seeped away. The channel, which runs for several miles, holds at most a foot or two of water. The authorities in London, horrified more by the expense of such public works than by their futility, cancelled the programme and resorted to soup kitchens as a belated effort to combat the famine, which had already done its worst.

The ravages of hunger and disease were mitigated in areas where the rural economy was not totally dependent on the ubiquitous potato. Ulster's thriving linen manufacture gave it the means to survive by purchasing adequate

This loom at the Ulster-American Folk Museum dates back to the days when linen was a thriving cottage industry.

food supplies at market prices. Although by the time of the famine linen production was already industrialized in Ulster, the eighteenth-century roots of the linen trade were entirely rural and domestic except for the final stages, which required heavy machinery. The cloth was sold unbleached to the drapers at the country linen markets; and these middlemen arranged for the bleaching and sale of the finished item. Dublin was the centre of the linen export trade and remained so until the end of the eighteenth century when there began that unstoppable concentration on Belfast.

The lot of the rural linen-weaver was relatively pleasant.

They were mostly self-employed, and it did not take much to lure them away from their looms. Hunting was their great passion; and there is a telling report of the love of the chase among the weavers of County Armagh: 'keeping packs of hounds, every man one, and joining: they hunt hares; a pack of hounds is never heard, but all the weavers leave their looms, and away they go after them by hundreds.' To judge by their houses, some of which have been reconstructed in the various heritage and folk-parks of Ireland, the weavers enjoyed a standard of living vastly superior to that of the miserable cottiers, whose only wealth lay in the cultivation of a rented potato bed. A weaver's house required good light for working at the loom; and so it was provided with many more windows than the byre houses and cabins. Generous fireplaces were also much in evidence, for a weaver could not perform the delicate tasks of his trade with numb fingers.

Linen manufacture from the harvesting of the flax to the finished product went through a variety of processes which provided much employment. After sowing and pulling of the flax, there was retting, scutching, hackling, spinning, winding, weaving, bleaching and beetling to be attended to. Beetling was the thickening of the cloth to give it its characteristic sheen, accomplished by a steady hammering of the rolls of cloth in specialized water-driven mills such as the one at Wellbrook in County Tyrone. Before chemical bleaching was introduced it was the usual practice to let nature do the job. The bolts of cloth were unrolled in huge lengths and left to lie beneath the sky on meadows known as bleach-greens. Here the action of the sunlight, even when diffused by clouds, brought about the desired whitening of the natural grey-brown colour of the material.

Let us not doubt the high monetary value of linen cloth, for the bleach-greens were watched over by look-outs who concealed themselves in circular stone huts which

The Wellbrook Beetling Mill, Co. Tyrone, used water power to hammer a sheen on to rolls of unbleached linen.

This watch tower at a bleaching green aimed to deter linen thieves. (Ulster Folk & Transport Museum.)

resembled the top section of the early monastic round towers. Spy-holes allowed the watchmen to keep a wary eye on the possible approach of any linen thieves. Those foolish enough to be caught stealing linen had to reckon with the ultimate punishment of the law; and the death sentence was regularly applied in such cases. Even receiving stolen linen was a hanging offence, and the death penalty for this misdemeanour was not repealed until 1811.

The rural Ireland that slowly emerged from the human wreckage of the famine years of the middle of the nineteenth century was essentially different to that which preceded them. In addition to the drastic depopulation there was also a radical restructuring of society. The cottier class had been decimated. Before the famine they had outnumbered tenant farmers by five to two, but within a couple of decades the ratio stood at one to one and was still falling. The statistics for the mud-cabins tell a similar tale. They declined from astronomic heights to just under 40,000 by 1871; and the overall figure for one-room houses on smallholdings had fallen to less than 4,000 by 1911. The vanishing human beings of Ireland in the second half of the nineteenth century left behind little trace of their existence on the landscape. Their makeshift dwellings, described in 1845 as 'a congeries of hovels

Rural Ireland was not without its charms, as may be seen at the Glencolumbkille Folk Village, Co. Donegal.

The rustic dwellings at Glencolumbkille are typical of what was once a widespread style of regional vernacular.

thrown indiscriminately together, as if they fell in a shower from the sky' soon fell into ruin and stood for a while as the 'tombs of a departed race'. However, the mud and straw of which they were made were soon absorbed back into the soil whence they had sprung. An organic cycle of life and death had been completed.

For those who remained, prospects were marginally better. There was more land for fewer people, so that holdings became larger and more efficient units. But local differences were extreme; and the remoter districts of the west in Kerry, Donegal and Connemara clung on to the old ways of subsistence farming and to traditional housing

The Mellon Homestead at the Ulster-American Folk Park shows that not all emigrants were driven by extreme poverty.

forms. Thatched cabins were until very recently a common sight in these areas, but they have now at last been superseded by modern bungalows which look like miniature viceregal lodges with their stately porticos. Isolated whitewashed houses with a roof of yellow thatch are still maintained by their owners, but picturesque groupings of old-style cabins are increasingly rare. One such may be found in the scattered townland of Glencolumbkille on the west coast of Donegal. So charming is the effect of these homespun dwellings that, inevitably, they have been turned into a folk-village; but happily their roots in the community have been retained.

Perhaps the most elusive and yet curiously tangible aspect of Ireland's rural heritage are the missing millions who managed to emigrate to the United States, Canada and Australia as well as to Britain. Those who embarked on the long sea voyages across the Atlantic often found themselves to be the human cargo of the notorious 'coffin ships', in which shipwreck and ship's fever amounted to a final, cruel cull of a population that had already endured such grievous suffering. With the departure of entire communities a silence infinitely more profound than that caused by the death of individuals was left behind. Peat fires in the cabins which had been kept smouldering on round the clock and throughout the year for decades and even centuries were allowed to burn out. The last wisps of aromatic smoke rose up into the thatch, and the hearths went cold. With that there went also the comforting sounds and music of the old Gaelic folklore. Bitter memories were taken away across the seas as if etched in the folk-mind.

Poverty, overpopulation and emigration had been significant factors in Ireland before the famine of the 1840s; and emigration continued thereafter to play a major role in the demography of the Irish countryside, creating in the process an Irish diaspora of tremendous international importance. The further draining caused by the drift towards the big cities of Dublin and Belfast, which was another marked feature of the closing decades of the nineteenth century, also helped to create that subsequent impression of rural Ireland as a series of lonely landscapes punctuated by the occasional cabin with the big houses sitting secretively in the middle of their large demesnes, well shielded from public view.

But even as we enjoy the peace and solitude of Irish life on the land, it is as well to be mindful of those many generations who, though long since decamped, once brought an animated human dimension to the natural

This simple memorial at Doolough, Co. Mayo, to victims of the famine would be equally relevant at many other locations.

scene. The people had a name for almost every feature of the landscape in their locality; and though these are still printed on the maps their intimate memory is becoming hazy. There were Masses in the open fields and schools in the shelter of the hedges, that were the result of poverty as much as of the penal laws. A traveller in Ireland in the 1770s wrote that he had observed 'many a ditchful of scholars'. Let us not be sentimentally nostalgic about such things, but simply be aware of their existence in the past. Rural Ireland today is full of such ghosts who have now joined the fairies as the guardian spirits of the countryside. Their cries and their laughter are borne in the wind which combs the long grass as if still searching for those who used to scratch a meagre living digging potatoes from the soil with their rustic spades.

Dromore Castle, Co. Limerick. Ireland's most amazing piece of Gothic Revival is now an empty shell, and inaccessible.

HOUSES OF THE ASCENDANCY – GOTHIC VISIONS

THE FIRST GLIMPSE of Dromore Castle can give you something of a culture shock. It's rather like discovering that Ludwig of Bavaria had built a secret retreat in the depths of County Limerick. The dramatic silhouette of the castle's fantasy skyline so delighted its architect Edward William Godwin that he took to contemplating it by moonlight and drawing sketches. Godwin had every reason to be proud of the splendid appearance of Dromore for he had diligently sought inspiration from the architecture of medieval and ancient Ireland such as the massing of buildings on the Rock of Cashel. Among the gables and battlements of Dromore Castle the conical form of what appears to be an early Christian round tower reaches for the sky. This is an archaeological reference of real thrust and impact which provides a powerful climax to a bold design. There are many other Gothic visions among the country homes of the nineteenth-century Irish Ascendancy, but Dromore is in a class of its own.

Its overwhelming effect had much to do with the personality of its patron, the third Earl of Limerick who was the President of the Architectural Society in London. The Earl, who inherited some 5700 acres in the counties of Cork and Limerick at the tender age of twenty-six, came from a family of absentee landlords, but he was determined to build himself an Irish residence that would reflect his ancestral roots as well as his status and fortune.

The time was the late 1860s, and the tide of full-blooded, medievalist architecture had been running for about fifty years and was still in full spate. Unlike many other 'castles' of the period Dromore was no sham but a serious production which contained many authentic features copied from original Irish castles of the Middle Ages. Crenellated battlements, loopholes and machicolations were realistic enough to give the impression that this was a proper fortress; and the walls were six feet thick with a pronounced batter at the base, which could in theory bounce projectiles released from the battlements right into the face of any assailants.

That the Earl of Limerick's defensive arrangements went perhaps beyond aristocratic whimsy is evidenced by a contemporary review in the influential *Building News* of 29 March 1867: 'the corridors are kept on the outer side of the building and all the entrances are well guarded, so that in the event of the country being disturbed the inmates of Dromore Castle might not only feel secure themselves but be able to give real shelter to others.' Indeed, agrarian and political unrest were very much in the air, although another fifty years were to pass before the burning of Ireland's country houses became something of a national sport.

In any event, the descendants of the Earl of Limerick no longer resided at Dromore Castle by that time, possibly discouraged by the all-pervasive damp which was so bad that Godwin's planned mural decorations could never be carried out. The property was later sold to a merchant family in Limerick who kept the place going until the 1950s. Thereafter, the interior was gutted as any valuable fittings and fixtures such as doors and windows were ripped out and sold for hard cash. Now roofless and forlorn, Dromore Castle is an empty shell. But such was the robust quality of the stonework that the external fabric has retained its outline and its capacity to impress. It is one of the most romantic ruins of nineteenth-century Ireland, and equal to the most extravagantly fanciful concepts of Victorian Britain as a whole.

Thomastown in County Tipperary, a vast fortified mansion built half a century earlier, had set the pace in Ireland for eccentric medievalist fantasies, but since its abandonment in 1872 it has declined into an ivy-clad ruin. Humewood Castle in County Wicklow of the late 1860s was a contemporary of Dromore; and it shared with it a skyline full of dramatic incident as well as several defensive features which gave its owner, the Right Honourable William Wentworth Fitzwilliam Dick of Humewood MP, a feeling of relative security in those troubled times. However, the builder had to sue both Mr Dick, as he was known for short, and the architect William White for settlement of his bill of £25,000, which was a modest sum according to the prevailing levels of expenditure on Irish country houses.

Shortage of funds resulted in one ambitiously conceived venture proceeding no further than its grandiloquent gatehouse. Ballysaggartmore in County Waterford was commenced with high hopes and great expectations in the 1820s by a Mr Arthur Keily, whose desire to impress the neighbours very soon outran his financial resources. He had only completed a turreted lodge and an avenue leading via a bridge to a gateway with

another Gothick lodge when his funds were exhausted. The bravado of the overture amounted to nothing but a pitiful anticlimax; and Mr and Mrs Keily, by now in straitened circumstances, were obliged to live on in their modest abode which was infinitely inferior to their magnificent gateway. The moral of the story is too obvious to bear repeating.

At Brittas Castle in County Tipperary it was the death of the owner Captain Henry Augustus Langley in 1834 which prevented his scheme for a comprehensive rebuilding of an ancient fortification advancing beyond the most imposing barbican. Captain Langley was killed by a piece of falling masonry as he supervised work on the site. His vision for an authentic reproduction of the Middle Ages was not shared by his heirs who called a halt to the work. Even in its unfinished state Brittas Castle is significant as a serious attempt to faithfully rebuild a medieval castle on its original foundations.

Another variation on the medieval theme was played at Gosford Castle in County Armagh which has the distinction of being the very first example in the British Isles of the style known as the Norman Revival. The architect entrusted with the task by the second Earl of Gosford was Thomas Hopper who took his Norman obsessions to even greater heights a few years later at Penrhyn in North Wales. Round arched doorways and windows combined with the square keep and circular towers to create a wonderful complex of buildings which are a perfect synthesis of Norman and Victorian architectural values, representing power, permanence and stature.

The same experience is on offer at Glenstal Castle in County Limerick which was commenced in 1837 for Sir Joseph Barrington. The work was interrupted during the famine years but was subsequently resumed with the Norman enthusiasm undiminished. The general massing of the building is similar to Gosford Castle, but Glenstal

Gosford Castle, Co. Armagh, by Thomas Hopper, was the first grand production of the Norman Revival in the nineteenth century.

offers in addition a wealth of striking features such as a full-scale copy of a most elaborate Hiberno-Romanesque doorway in Killaloe Cathedral as well as several motifs borrowed from Clonmacnoise. The front door of Glenstal is flanked by statues of Edward I and Eleanor of Castile. Culturally discordant and anachronistic in a typically Victorian way is the scroll with the words *'Cead Mile Fáilte'* which Eleanor is holding. Evidently, the first promoters of the Celtic Revival saw nothing incongruous in portraying a Spanish-born Queen of England as a symbolic bearer of the traditional Irish greeting of welcome.

Lismore Castle in County Waterford had no need for

Lismore Castle, Co. Waterford, was a medievalist vision of the 6th Duke of Devonshire, and built with no expense spared.

bogus connections with the monarchs of medieval England, standing as it does on the site of a castle built by King John in 1185; but its present architectural appearance has none the less all the characteristics of that sham medievalism so beloved of the Victorian age. Lismore had passed through a variety of owners and occupants including the roguish Archbishop of Cashel Myler Magrath, Sir Walter Ralegh, and Richard Boyle, the first Earl of Cork. The latter had extensively rebuilt and updated the ancient pile in his favourite Renaissance manner. In this guise it passed by the marriage of the sole surviving daughter and heiress of the fourth Earl of Cork into the possession of the Cavendish family of the Dukes of Devonshire who still own it. It was the sixth Duke of Devonshire, succeeding to the title in 1811, who was responsible for the Gothic remodelling of Lismore Castle over a period of almost fifty years until his death in 1858. To him we owe the picturesque composition of turrets and battlements faced with stone cut from the Duke's own quarries near the ancestral seat of Chatsworth in Derbyshire. Unlike men of lesser substance, the Duke of Devonshire was able to complete Lismore to his own demanding standards. The ballroom, fashioned from the previous chapel, bears the unmistakable imprint of the Pugin style, which stood in the vanguard of the Gothic Revival.

A comparable mix of the genuinely medieval with a Renaissance overlay confronted the nineteenth Earl of Ormonde (elevated to Marquess in 1825) at the family home of Kilkenny Castle. The first stone castle on the site had been built by Strongbow's son-in-law William, the Earl Marshal from 1192; and it was the illustrious first Duke of Ormonde who had endeavoured in the seventeenth century to make the castle look less like of an antique. However, architectural fashion had turned full circle two centuries later when Kilkenny Castle assumed the face that is familiar today. Then the prevailing taste

The long gallery at Kilkenny Castle was a grandiose scheme in the best tradition of Victorian historicism.

demanded a convincing castellated exterior as well as a comfortable interior in tune with Victorian ideas of domestic refinement. Accordingly, the design brief was described by a contemporary visitor as 'modernized within and unmodernized without'.

Thus the Duke of Ormonde's artistic efforts were undone, but for the entrance gateway, as Kilkenny Castle reassumed its martial character, adopting a watchful stance over the neighbouring city. Of the interiors, the Picture Gallery – 150 feet long and 27 feet wide – is a brilliant demonstration of Victorian style, combining advanced technology with artful historicism. The 30-foot-high roof is partly glazed to admit a perfectly diffused light conducive to the appreciation of the pictures; but at the same time it imitates the ancient hammerbeam principle and is decorated with a profusion of motifs which amount to a revivalist extravaganza. Here again, we may perceive the early signs of the Celtic Revival, notably in the forms and patterns which suggest a whole range of cultural associations from La Tène and Norse to Pre-Raphaelite. This is the real stuff of High Victorian design, a heady concoction in which the individual ingredients have been mysteriously transformed to create an effect that was both excitingly new and reassuringly old at the same time: progress and nostalgia in a curious symbiosis. A final eclectic note is struck by a Moorish staircase: orientalism in league with medievalism to cap it all!

But not all the Gothic-inspired country houses of nineteenth-century Ireland were grand productions of castle-like pretensions. The style known as Neo-Tudor or Elizabethan, which endeavoured to copy the cosier domesticity of the English sixteenth-century manor house, was ideally suited to the practical requirements of daily life on a more modest budget. The trend may be traced back to the 1820s with the Earl of Meath's comely Kilruddery in County Wicklow. And an instructive juxta-position of the style and its medieval predecessor may be gained at Narrow Water Castle in County Down. The name is shared by two contrasting structures. By the waterfront there is a typical tower-house of the late Middle Ages, and a short distance away up the hill a new house was built in the 1830s in the guise of a Neo-Tudor mansion. It was described in 1837 as 'a very fine edifice in the Elizabethan style'; and it showed that it wasn't necessary to ape a castle in order to cut a very fine figure indeed.

Carrigglas Manor in County Longford, commenced in 1837 and thereby asserting a claim to be Ireland's first

Narrow Water Castle, Co. Down, one of the most impressive productions in the style of the Tudor Revival.

truly Victorian Gothic house, represents a strange blend of house and castle, combining mullioned and transomed windows and homely gables with mock battlements and angular towers. Muckross House near Killarney in County Kerry is unambiguous in its Elizabethan identity, having no defensive delusions whatsoever. It was built in 1843 for a certain Mr Henry Arthur Herbert MP, a man of substance who could trace back his roots to the squires of the Welsh Marches. However, the Herbert family's prosperity did not outlast the nineteenth century. A sharp decline in their finances led to the appointment of trustees, and eventually in 1899 to the sale of Muckross House to Lord Ardilaun of the Guinness dynasty. He in turn sold it on in 1910 to a Mr and Mrs William Bowers Bourn of California, who thought that the Muckross estate of 11,000 acres would make a handsome wedding gift for their daughter Maud and future son-in-law Mr Arthur Vincent.

During its Victorian heyday Muckross House was visited by the great and the good, including Queen Victoria and Prince Albert in 1861. With its wild outlook on to the rugged splendour of the Macgillycuddy Reeks, the loftiest peaks in Ireland, Muckross offered the *ne plus ultra* of the Victorian country house experience: snug luxury within, and a prospect of raw nature at its most spectacular without. When Maud died in 1929 she bequeathed Muckross House together with the entire estate to the Irish nation in yet another of the acts of American generosity to Ireland which were fast becoming a national tradition.

It was also through an American benefactor that Glenveagh Castle in County Donegal at last found its way into public ownership when in 1975 its proprietor Mr Henry McIlhenny, a third-generation Irish-American, donated the mock-medieval castle and gardens to the people of Ireland. Like Muckross House, it is now the centre of a

Muckross House near Killarney in Co. Kerry was a romantic retreat with a glorious prospect of rugged nature.

The view from Glenveagh Castle, Co. Donegal, takes in some of the wildest scenery in the whole of Ireland.

National Park. This was indeed a fortunate ending, but the earlier history of the Glenveagh Estate had been far from happy for those who resided on it around the middle of the nineteenth century. The trouble began in 1857 when John George Adair, the son of a gentleman farmer in County Laois, began to build up a sizeable estate in Donegal with large-scale purchases of land through the Encumbered Estates Court. Adair did invest huge sums in developing his land, but he soon revealed a penchant for harassing the tenants over hunting rights. Before long a mutual animosity boiled over into a frontal collision of interests. Tempted by the lucrative rewards of sheep-farming, Adair resolved to clear the tenants by summarily evicting them from their cabins. The meticulous reporting of the 'Glenveagh Evictions' in the *Londonderry Standard* narrated some harrowing details, ending with the sad observation: 'There these poor starving people remain on the cold bleak mountains, no one caring for them whether they live or die. 'Tis horrible to think of, but more horrible to behold.'

John George Adair did not have to pay for the consequences of his cruelty, for in 1867 he married a wealthy American widow Cornelia Ritchie. He then built his baronial Glenveagh Castle in the middle of a by then depopulated landscape. But he soon lost interest in Donegal, and like so many of those whom he had evicted he emigrated to the United States. However, he owned a majority share in an enormous Texan ranch. He died in America in 1885.

Another Irish landlord, Major Denis Mahon of Strokestown Park in County Roscommon, was not so lucky. He inherited his estate just as the spectre of the famine loomed large. To add to the problems, there were already rent arrears of £13,000 which had accumulated and were impossible to collect. Major Mahon decided to clear the estate of impecunious and starving tenants by offering

Strokestown Park House, Co. Roscommon, was at the centre of tragic events in 1847 in the aftermath of the famine.

them passages on two chartered vessels to North America. Apparently, the word got about that one of the vessels had foundered with the loss of all crew and passengers. That the rumour gained instant credence is not surprising, for many of the ships used for the transport of Ireland's destitute masses were the unsea- worthy 'coffin ships' of the old days of the slave trade. In fact, one of the ships had been forced to turn back as a result of bad weather and later resumed its voyage to Quebec, and both eventually arrived safely. However, the correct version of events came too late to save Major Mahon who was shot, ostensibly as an act of reprisal, as

Ashford Castle, Co. Mayo. The baronial bridge is a fitting introduction to this castellated mansion, now a hotel.

he returned to Strokestown Park on 2 November 1847 after a meeting in Roscommon to discuss the relief programme. A significant contributing factor to his murder was almost certainly the eviction of tenants carried out by the land agent John Ross Mahon on the Major's behalf.

The Earl of Leitrim received what even some other Irish landlords considered to be no more than his just deserts when he was shot dead on 2 April 1878; but not all estate owners were heartless usurers and evictors. The Duke of Leinster and the Marquess of Waterford were among those held in high esteem. Indeed, some Ascendancy landlords bankrupted themselves through non-collection of rents and mortgaging their estates to feed the starving at the height of the famine. The Guinness family acquired an enduring reputation for paternalistic care and concern. At the same time Sir Arthur Guinness (later Lord Ardilaun) represented the epitome of the new breed of nineteenth-century magnates, deriving their enormous revenues from industry rather than agricultural rents. The Guinness baronial pile of Ashford Castle in County Mayo is thus a monument to the profits of brewing stout rather than the traditional income of the country gentleman. This prestigious castellated mansion, built by 1870, was one of the last of the big Gothic country houses of Ireland.

Birr Castle in County Offaly had already been extended in the Gothick mode so beloved of late eighteenth-century taste, but it was not for their architectural achievements that the nineteenth-century Earls of Rosse, the masters of Birr, earned for themselves a very special place in the ranks of Ascendancy families. William, the third Earl of Rosse, studied mathematics and astronomy, and after a spell as MP for King's County from 1823 to 1834, he turned his full energies exclusively towards celestial exploration. Birr Castle became Ireland's first space observatory. The Earl's plans were nothing if not grandiose; for he constructed on his demesne at Birr a gigantic telescope with a 72-inch reflector. The mirror itself weighed all of 4 tons, and the tube was so huge that it resembled the barrel of some outlandish piece of artillery. A housing of solid masonry was required to support it; and this was designed in the Gothic mode to match the style of Birr Castle. From a distance, the heavily buttressed structure looks like one of those follies which were so popular as eye-catchers in aristocratic parks.

However, like many grand Victorian schemes in Ireland and elsewhere, the Giant of Birr or the Leviathan – as the super-telescope was known – did not quite fulfil the expectations of its creator. For one thing, it was so bulky that it could be moved only a few degrees in one segment

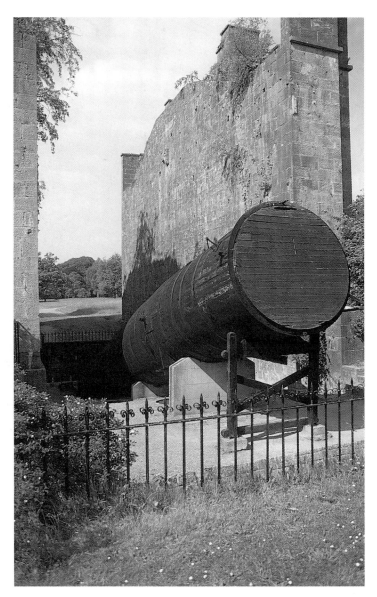

The Giant of Birr – the great telescope of the Earls of Rosse – now stares out blankly in Birr Castle Demesne, Co. Offaly.

Johnstown Castle, Co. Wexford, strikes a picturesque posture by its ornamental lake. It is now a research centre.

of the heavens; and for another, the heavens themselves were all too often obscured by the omnipresent Irish clouds and mists rolling in from the Atlantic. Nevertheless, the fourth Earl of Rosse continued his father's obsession, and on clear nights he recorded in a series of wondrously executed sketches his observations of spiral nebulae. He took special pleasure in walking favoured house guests through the tube of the Leviathan where they would pose for pictures. The Giant of Birr now slumbers on like a dinosaur in the long grass of the stately demesne, looking somewhat abandoned, now bereft of its 72-inch reflector which found its way in 1908 to the Science Museum in London.

While Birr's scientific career is now over, that of

another Irish castle has only just begun. Johnstown Castle in County Wexford, one of the most picturesque compositions of its kind, has become a research centre for the Department of Agriculture. It is a use that would have pleased one of its nineteenth-century owners, H. K. Grogan-Morgan, who was generally acknowledged to be 'adept in chemical science' and who built a small laboratory in what was once the ballroom wing of the house.

Kylemore Castle in County Galway arose as the result of a personal whim of a young lady. The story goes that the immensely wealthy Manchester financier Mr Mitchell Henry was enjoying his Irish honeymoon in the summer of 1852 in this remote part of romantic Connemara. During a picnic luncheon by the lough at Kylemore his beautiful bride Margaret sighed that she would so like to live there at that majestic spot so far from everywhere. The only building for miles around was a modest shooting-box: all else was a natural paradise of moor and mountain. Knowing the resources of her husband, Margaret might have suspected that her wish could be turned into a reality. And so it was to be, although it was more than ten years later that Mr Mitchell Henry purchased the shooting-box which came with an estate comprising 9,000 acres of the wildest scenery of Connemara.

What then ensued went far beyond the realm of a casual daydream. Between 1864 and 1868 there arose in this deserted landscape not an occasional retreat but a Gothic palace with thirty-three bedrooms, a ballroom, a Turkish bath and a chapel along with the usual morning room, breakfast room, dining-room, drawing-room and so forth. How the family planned to live here so cut off from the rest of the world and their vital business interests is hard to fathom. Even finding workers in the locality was a problem; and the economic benefits of Kylemore Castle spread themselves over a huge area as labour was hired for its construction.

Kylemore Abbey, Co. Galway, began life as a fantasy castle for the wife of a rich industrialist. It is now a school.

The opulence of Kylemore may be judged by this lavishly carved marble fireplace in a reception room.

Perhaps it would have been better for Mr Mitchell Henry if he had given more thought to his commercial activities, for the final bill for Kylemore came to a phenomenal £1.25 million. Then personal disaster struck when his wife died during a visit to Egypt, and thereafter his financial wizardry started to fail him. Finally, he was obliged to find a buyer for his dream castle, which was described in the sales brochure of 1902 in the following terms: 'lavish expenditure of a beneficent owner whose princely fortune transformed a once insignificant sporting lodge into one of the most stately homes existent in the British Isles'. For once the estate agent's blurb was not overstated.

A Mr Zimmerman from Chicago relieved Mr Henry of the property for a fraction of what it had originally cost. He thought it would make a rather special wedding present for his daughter, who was marrying into the British aristocracy in the person of the Duke of Manchester. In 1913 the spendthrift Duke mortgaged Kylemore and the castle was abandoned to its fate. However, there was soon to be a happy ending, for Kylemore was acquired by the Irish Abbey of the Nuns of St Benedict which had lost its house at Ypres during the Great War of 1914–18. The Benedictine nuns are still in residence, and the establishment is run as a girls' boarding-school. It appears ideally suited for its purpose, and the erotic carvings on the Carrara marble fireplace in the reception room do not appear to trouble anyone. Kylemore Castle has found its true destiny as Kylemore Abbey.

There was one other minor theme to make an appearance among the Gothic visions of nineteenth-century Ireland. The style known as Scottish Baronial had been given a tremendous boost by Victoria and Albert's remodelling of Balmoral Castle. The wild landscapes of Ireland also received a number of buildings which paid tribute to the same idea. Blarney Castle House of 1874 was

Belfast Castle acquired this stylish external staircase during the Indian summer of the Baronial fashion.

erected near the more famous medieval castle and decorated with the stepped gables and conical turrets which are the hallmarks of Scottish Baronial. Another fine specimen had been built a few years earlier in 1870 for the third Marquess of Donegall. This was Belfast Castle, which occupies a dominant position worthy of the family who had once owned the whole of Belfast. Like many others of their kind, the Donegalls had been notorious as profligate absentee landlords, and the second Marquess had left behind debts in excess of £400,000. The construction of Belfast Castle had been possible only thanks to the financial guarantees of the wealthy Lord Ashley, who married into the family. The castle's most splendid feature is an ornate external staircase of snake-like sinuosity, added in 1894 as a final flourish.

As the political temperature rose in Ireland in the opening decades of the twentieth century leading to the establishment of the Irish Free State, so the houses of the Ascendancy came to be seen increasingly as the residences of a doomed aristocracy and as symbols of past injustices. During the Troubles of 1920–3 many became the target of reprisals, and some two hundred of Ireland's estimated two thousand country houses were burned at this time. It would be wrong, however, to ascribe every ruined shell of a stately home in the Irish countryside to the work of the arsonists, for many of the great houses fell victim to the changed economic circumstances of their owners. Many are the tales of threadbare Ascendancy landlords eking out a miserable existence as their houses slowly collapsed over their heads. We read of one old gentleman moving from room to room as the rain penetrated one corner of his residence after another, and of an elderly couple reduced to sleeping in the drawing-room in order to save on the fuel bills. *Sic transit gloria mundi.*

Belfast's City Hall in Donegall Square symbolises the city at the peak of its fortunes as an industrial metropolis.

LINENOPOLIS – BELFAST BOOMTIME

TAKE A STROLL round Belfast's Donegall Square, and you might easily imagine yourself to be in an industrial city such as Manchester or Liverpool. The centre of the square is occupied by a monumental Baroque wedding-cake of a building, the City Hall of 1906 which symbolizes the zenith of municipal pride in this, the most meteoric of late-Victorian cities in the British Isles. The west flank of the square is dominated by the Edwardian bombast of the Scottish Provident Institution of 1902 which – in the words of one architectural commentator – 'glowers massively' at the City Hall, as if asserting the pre-eminence of Capital over Corporation as the underlying message of Belfast's success. To the east stands the once imposing, but now relatively modest Classical portico of the Donegall Square Methodist Church of 1834, serving as a benchmark of the lesser aspirations prevailing at the outset of Belfast's sensational period of growth. The main entrance of the City Hall on the north side of the square looks out on to the majestic figure of Queen Victoria carved in stone, proud and regal like the figurehead of a stately galleon.

The inevitable comparisons with the industrial conurbations of northern England, and even more so with Glasgow, contain the key to the understanding of the essential character of Belfast. The impetus to the phenomenal boom of nineteenth-century Belfast may be traced back to the huge influx of Scottish Presbyterians into Ulster in the late seventeenth and early eighteenth centuries. It was hardly surprising that these people subsequently took their lead from the industrial revolution that was occurring on mainland Britain; and it was almost inevitable that Belfast should seek not only to emulate but to outshine its British counterparts. The resulting foreignness of Belfast in its Irish context was remarked on by many contemporary observers. A Mr and Mrs Hall made the comment on its appearance in 1843 that it was 'decidedly un-national. That it is in Ireland but not of it is a remark ever on the lips of visitors from south or west.' H. D. Inglis was even more emphatic: 'the town and its neighbouring districts have nothing in common with the rest of Ireland.'

Just how closely the shaping of Belfast was linked to the mainstream of urban and industrial development in Britain may be seen in the seminal event which set the whole business in motion. In the year 1777 Robert Joy embarked on a journey through England and Scotland with a specific view to borrowing ideas for gainful employment which might be followed by the inmates of the Poor House in Belfast. His son Henry recorded that he 'conceived the scheme of introducing into this then

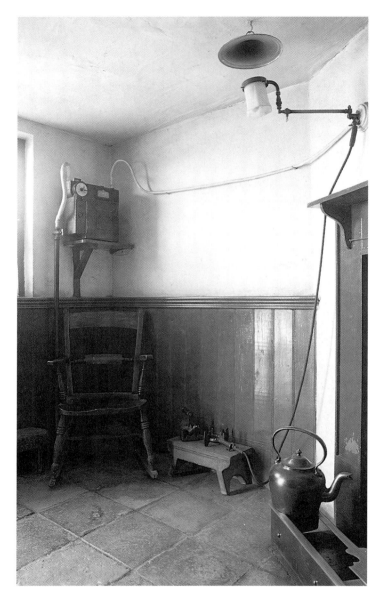

There is not much sign of homespun comfort in this Belfast interior from Tea Lane. (Ulster Folk & Transport Museum.)

desponding Kingdom, the most intricate Branches of the Cotton Manufacture which had proved unfailing sources of Industry and Opulence to our sister country'. As a result of Joy's initiative, cotton was king in Belfast for the next half-century, and the work to be had on the looms and spinning jennies sucked in tens of thousands of destitute folk from the surrounding countryside. The population rose from 13,000 in 1782 to 20,000 in 1800; and then it leapt to more than 70,000 by 1841. An unstoppable bandwagon was rolling which was soon to be a juggernaut.

Although cotton brought industrialization to Belfast, it was linen which turned the town into a city, and the city into a metropolis which fully merited its nickname of 'Linenopolis'. Belfast had already emerged by the end of the eighteenth century as a major export centre for linen, whose manufacture was still both rural and domestic in nature. In 1783 it had posted its challenge to Dublin by laying the foundation stone of the White Linen Hall. This was the building, a functional two-storey structure around a large quadrangle, which was later demolished to provide a site for the City Hall in Donegall Square. However, not until it was possible to apply power-spinning to flax did linen production become the powerhouse of Belfast's industrialization. The wet-spinning process, developed in Leeds in 1825, paved the way for the rapid metamorphosis of Belfast; and it made its entrance in the most dramatic and symbolic of manners.

In 1828 Mulholland's cotton mill went up in an almighty conflagration, and the owners took advantage of the situation to assess the viability of going over to the power-spinning of flax. It was an instant success. The new mill in York Street rapidly grew into a world leader with 25,000 spindles. Nor was the lesson lost on other Belfast textile manufacturers. A contemporary observer described the situation, not without irony: 'Several of the far-seeing merchants of the Northern Athens began to surmise the truth respecting the new El Dorado that had been discovered in York Street, and no long time elapsed until other tall chimneys began to rise in different parts of the town.' Linen was thus the industry which launched Belfast into the super-league. In spite of the occasional spectacular slump in the market the 'linen lords' of the city repeatedly made 'profitable returns of well nigh fabulous percentage'.

Heavy engineering and shipbuilding added further to the rags-to-riches saga. Some of the ships which went down the slipway of the Harland & Wolff shipyard for the White Star Line epitomized the exuberance of the wealthy merchants of Belfast. A high point was reached in 1899 with the launch of the *Oceanic II*, then the biggest ship in the world. It was described as 'a sybaritic ship' and 'a Hotel Cecil afloat'. Perhaps the launch of the ill-fated *Titanic* in 1912 can be seen in retrospect as a doom-laden omen, marking the beginning of Belfast's long and painful decline.

But the possibility of serious economic collapse cannot have entered the minds of the Belfast city fathers as their brave new 'Linenopolis' went from strength to strength in the second half of the nineteenth century. Just as growth was slowing down elsewhere in the longer-established industrial cities, so Belfast turned on an extra burst of speed, like a sprinter heading for the tape which was marked with the year 1900, the conclusion of the most concentrated outpouring of productive energy that the world had ever seen. The city population jumped from just over 87,000 in 1851 to almost 175,000 in 1871, and then to a staggering 350,000 soon after the turn of the century. Things reached a climactic crescendo in the 1890s when the population of Belfast rose by more than one-third. Most of the growth was fuelled by immigration from rural Ireland, a factor which has made Belfast a

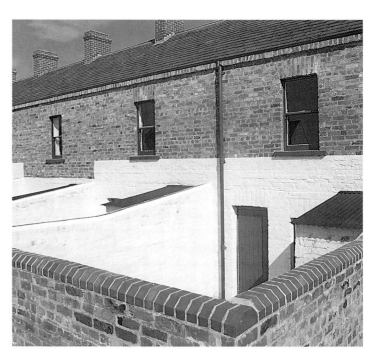

The backyards of Belfast were a world removed from Ireland's countryside, whence the city's workforce was now drawn.

microcosm in urban form of the country as a whole.

Sectarian tensions were already apparent at this time as the Protestant and Catholic newcomers took up their positions in separate neighbourhoods. Despite the over-crowding this was to be no melting pot. However, such was the frenetic work rate of Belfast that the overall success story determined the optimistic and expansion-istic mood of the place. Each new achievement was held up as an object of pride and admiration. The introduction of gas-lighting as early as 1823 was described in the *Belfast News-Letter* in terms of reverence: 'The light now used is the purest kind, shedding on the streets a brilliant

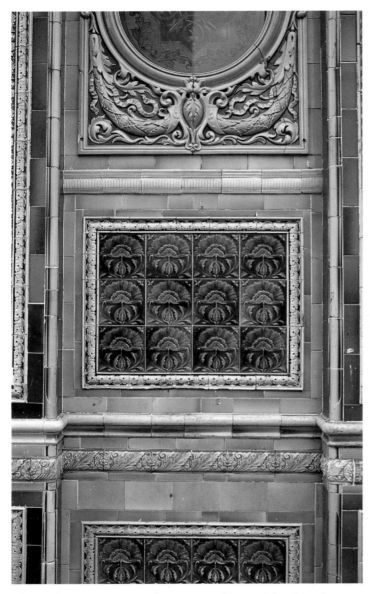

The High Victorian taste for ornate effect and bright colours is apparent at the Crown Liquor Saloon, Belfast.

lustre – pleasing but not dazzling – and more resembling the clear effulgence of a cloudless atmosphere illumined by the moon, than any artificial beams heretofore produced by the imitative power of man.' A similar sensation was generally felt when the first electric tram went into service in 1905. Meanwhile, horse-drawn trams and steam railways had encouraged the growth of salubrious suburbs. An advertisement of 1903 for the Cliftonville Garden Colony proclaimed: 'It costs only a penny from the Junction, and you will see some of the prettiest villas that have been erected since Noah left the Ark.'

In 1895 came the jewel in the crown – the Grand Opera House. The dazzling Oriental fantasy interior by Frank Matcham was one of the wonders of the city. It was contained within a grandly ostentatious building which has recently been refurbished. Just opposite it is the Crown Liquor Saloon of about 1885, the finest surviving example of Belfast's opulent gin palaces. Even a public house in late Victorian Belfast was deemed worthy of palatial treatment. Against all the odds, the National Trust has restored this proud relic of Belfast's heyday, and it is still in business.

The city abounds – despite the destruction of the Blitz and redevelopment – in exciting pieces of nineteenth-century architecture. Not surprisingly, banks rank highly among the finest buildings of their period, but public institutions have bequeathed an impressive body of major works. The Albert Memorial Clock Tower, St Malachy's Cathedral (Roman Catholic), Queen's University, the Custom House, St Anne's Cathedral (Church of Ireland) and the May Street Presbyterian Church provide the principal landmarks and illustrate the dominant themes of Victorian urban architecture in all its fulsome variety. The Palm House in the Botanic Gardens is worthy of special mention because it demonstrates the pioneering role of Belfast in applying new technology. It was a Dublin

The Crown Liquor Saloon remains one of the most evocative spots in Belfast to savour the mood of a century ago.

iron-founder, Richard Turner, who developed the art of curved iron ribs supporting curved glass; but his skills were put to work in 1839 in Belfast before the conservatories of Dublin's Glasnevin and London's Kew Gardens.

However surprising some may find it today to discover Belfast setting the pace in so many aspects of progress, its citizens of one hundred years ago had probably come to regard the pre-eminence of their city as self-evident.

The Palm House in Belfast's Botanic Gardens was in the vanguard of the glass and iron building technology in 1839.

When Belfast officially achieved city status in 1888 the Corporation decided that its newly built Town Hall of 1871 in Victoria Street was not prestigious or prominent enough to reflect the importance of the place. Negotiations were initiated with the Countess of Shaftesbury leading to the purchase and demolition of the White Linen Hall. The new City Hall on Donegall Square came in at £360,000, or more than twice the original budget. Few people batted an eyelid at this lavish overspending. The important thing was that Belfast acquired a focal point every bit as splendid as its economic achievements merited. It communicates a powerful message of success and prosperity.

But for all the magnificence there was, of course, a dark side to the glories of 'Linenopolis'. The linen industry had yielded vast profits, but at the expense of the workers who were among the poorest paid of all. The health hazards of flax dust on the lung and the dangers of mutilation from unprotected machinery made the workplace a perpetual risk to life and limb. Things were just as bad in the jerry-built workers' housing, where insanitary conditions and overcrowding exacted a heavy toll in human fatalities. A walk down the back streets and side alleys of nineteenth-century Belfast would have provided a shocking spectacle of suffering humanity.

The Rev. W. M. O'Hanlon documented the abject circumstances of the Belfast slum-dwellers in a series of graphic descriptions. One such, written in 1852, recorded the horror of the lives wasted away in the process of creating the urban splendours:

> But, plunging into the alleys and entries of this neighbourhood, what indescribable scenes of poverty, filth and wretchedness everywhere meet the eye. Barrack-lane was surely built when it was imagined the world would soon prove too strait for the number of its

inhabitants. About five or six feet is the space here allotted for the passage of the dwellers, and for the pure breath of heaven to find access to their miserable abodes. But, in truth, no pure breath of heaven ever enters here; it is tainted and loaded by the most noisome, recking feculance.

Under such conditions the ravages of fever and disease periodically spread like wildfire.

The higher wages of the engineering and shipbuilding sectors led to the construction of superior terraces of workers' housing, whose neat red-brick rows provide one of the characteristic images of Belfast today. Shipbuilding was to outlast linen manufacture and to give Belfast its definitive identity, so memorably expressed by the poet Louis MacNeice:

See Belfast, devout and profane and hard,
Built on reclaimed mud, hammers playing
    in the shipyard;
Time punched with holes like a steel sheet, time
Hardening the faces, veneering with a grey and
    speckled rime
The faces under the shawls and caps.

Humble terraces such as this at Tea Lane were once the norm in nineteenth century Belfast. (Ulster Folk & Transport Museum.)

Daniel O'Connell portrayed addressing one of the monster meetings which established his political reputation.

EMANCIPATION AND INDEPENDENCE

THE 120 YEARS from the Act of Union of 1800 until the Government of Ireland Act of 1920, which established the Irish Free State and the separate province of Northern Ireland, were among the most traumatic in the whole history of Ireland. Popular unrest, government coercion and mutual acts of violence punctuated this unhappy period, which was further convulsed by the cataclysm of the famine years of the 1840s. Starvation, emigration and a drift to the cities drained the countryside of millions of its people. With their loss the Irish language withered away, and almost died. By the middle of the nineteenth century already only 25 per cent of the population could still speak Irish, and a mere 5 per cent spoke it as their only language. Against this troubled background Ireland moved inexorably but fitfully towards a partial resolution of her various problems. However, there was to be no great single event such as the French Revolution to change the political landscape overnight and for all time. Instead, Ireland became periodically ungovernable through any number of uprisings and protests against British rule, some of which were destined to be glorious failures that later bore unexpected fruit. Out of the overall confusion and fragmentation of effort a number of charismatic figures stand out with superhuman clarity; and we may still encounter them at various places in Ireland which powerfully evoke their memory.

A favourite halt on the scenic circuit of south-west Ireland is the Derrynane National Historic Park. This beautiful and somnolent corner of County Kerry contains the ancestral home of the great Daniel O'Connell, affectionately known as 'Swaggering Dan', who was without doubt the best-loved and most universal in his message of those who dedicated themselves to the cause of Irish nationhood. His doctrine of non-violence, scrupulously adhered to by his followers, puts O'Connell in the same category as Mahatma Gandhi and Martin Luther King. Indeed, preceding both by a full one hundred years, O'Connell may be acclaimed as the pioneer in modern times among leaders who brought about political change through the peaceful mobilization of the masses. 'Human blood is no cement for the temple of liberty,' he wrote; and he meant it.

O'Connell came from a Catholic landowning family which had managed, despite the Penal Laws, to cling on both to its property and its religion. Derrynane House eventually passed to him in 1825, and though recently restored is still essentially in the shape and form given to it by O'Connell. One end of the drawing-room of Derrynane House is dominated by an oil painting depicting the 'Liberator', as he was also known, addressing a multitude of followers out in the countryside. These gatherings in the open air were O'Connell's way both of broadcasting

O'Connell's statue in Dublin is a national monument and a prominent landmark in the heart of the Irish capital.

his message and of demonstrating to the authorities the huge weight of public support behind him. His first political objective was the achievement of Catholic Emancipation in 1829 which permitted Irish Catholics to sit for the first time as MPs in the parliament at Westminster and to occupy a number of public posts previously withheld. This momentous victory was tainted, however, by the raising of the property qualification from £2 to £10, which effectively disenfranchised the vast majority of the rural population. Nevertheless, there was both in theory and practice an equality of parliamentary opportunity between Protestant and Catholic in Ireland.

Thereafter, O'Connell's 'monster meetings', as they were called by the London *Times*, concentrated on the more radical aim of the repeal of the Union with Britain. A rising tide of people power was reflected in the numbers who surged to hear the resonant voice of the 'Liberator', described by one who attended: 'You'd hear it a mile off, as if it was coming through honey.' Powerful it must have been, for an estimated three-quarters of a million converged in 1843 on the Hill of Tara to hear him. The entire proceedings were conducted with order and dignity, a phenomenon which the authorities found infinitely more disturbing than an armed riot. Official pressure was then brought to bear on O'Connell to cancel at the eleventh hour what would have been the biggest 'monster meeting' of them all, scheduled for 5 October 1843 at Clontarf, where in the year 1014 the Irish High King Brian Boru had put an end to the Viking dominion over Ireland. The symbolism of the place was felt to be too provocative and dangerous by the military and political masters in Dublin Castle who ordered O'Connell to call it off.

O'Connell's compliance was not out of weakness but stemmed from his principle of remaining within the law and from his resolve to do nothing that would undermine his ideal of non-violence. He was, none the less, arrested for his pains and held for a short while. In 1844, under extremely volatile circumstances, he calmed the mood of the country with his famous proclamation: 'I tell you solemnly that your Enemies, and the Enemies of Ireland are desirous that there should be a breaking out of Tumult, Riot or other outrage. Be you therefore perfectly peaceable ... obey my advice. No Riot, no Tumult, no Blow, no Violence.' The human character and warmth of personality which lay behind these words may be better experienced in the soft and pastoral setting of the family home at Derrynane, his native earth, than at the grander public monument in Dublin's O'Connell Street or the austere round tower in the cemetery at Glasnevin which marks the place where his body was laid to rest.

Death caught up with 'Swaggering Dan' in 1847 at Genoa where he was *en route* to sunnier climes on the advice of his doctors. His last wishes were that his body be brought back to Ireland but that his heart should be taken out and sent for burial in Rome. His final years had been clouded by the horrors of the famine. 'A nation is starving,' he told the House of Commons, 'Ireland is in your hands ... if you do not save her, she cannot save herself.' A later Prime Minister, William Ewart Gladstone, described O'Connell in the most glowing terms: 'Almost from the opening of my Parliamentary life I felt that he was the greatest popular leader whom the world had ever seen.' More than a hundred years later the memory and message of Daniel O'Connell have lost none of their relevance, and not only within the context of Ireland.

At Avondale in County Wicklow there stands an elegant Georgian mansion which was the birthplace and home of that other towering individual of nineteenth-century Irish politics, Charles Stewart Parnell. Parnell took over where O'Connell had left off, for he devoted his considerable talents and energies to a resolution of the land question and the struggle for Home Rule. His origins

O'Connell's body was laid to rest in a vault beneath a round tower in Dublin's Glasnevin Cemetery.

demonstrate one of the paradoxes of Irish history, namely that some of the most prominent of nationalists had their roots in the alien landlord class of the Protestant Ascendancy. Parnell's ancestors had come to Ireland from Cheshire in the seventeenth century, but quickly came to associate themselves with Ireland while remaining staunchly Protestant. An American grandfather, who had fought as an admiral against the British navy, possibly gave Parnell a streak of militancy lacking in O'Connell; but Parnell was a man committed to the political process, who exploited to the full the opportunities of a hung British parliament to further the cause of Home Rule. In the

Liberal leader Gladstone he found a counterpart who was more than willing to let Parnell's Home Rule MPs exert their formidable pressure on a reluctant House of Commons. Gladstone had declared early in his career: 'My mission is to pacify Ireland.' His portrait was revered by some but was an object of desecration for others, used to decorate the bottom of many a chamber-pot in the country houses up and down the land.

As a landowner himself, Parnell understood that the protection of tenants' rights was a necessary and attainable goal, which would do much to bring immediate relief to the suffering of the poorest countryfolk. Home Rule, on the other hand, would inevitably take longer. A degree of success was marked by the passing of the Land Act in 1870, though its provisions were substantially weakened by the House of Lords, dominated as it was by the owners of great estates. A second and further-reaching Land Act was passed in 1881. The first real chance for Home Rule came five years later in 1886 when Gladstone had to rely on the eighty-six MPs of the Irish Home Rule Party in order to form a government. Unfortunately, the issue split the Liberals; and after defeat at the ensuing general election, Gladstone was out of office.

By this time Parnell was the undisputed champion of the Irish cause. His brief incarceration in Kilmainham Jail had immeasurably enhanced his national stature, giving him a degree of popular support previously withheld. In 1890 his standing on both sides of the Irish Sea was at an all-time high when the scandal of his love affair with Mrs Katherine O'Shea broke suddenly over his head. The formerly complaisant husband Captain William O'Shea MP had decided to file for divorce, citing Parnell as co-respondent. A decade of adultery was thereby exposed to public view. Merciless Victorian morality did the rest. Parnell was disowned by his supporters as well as denounced by his opponents. He fought on nevertheless

Parnell's portrait surveys the comfortable scene of the family home at Avondale, Co. Wicklow.

to rehabilitate himself and attempted to win back the leadership he had lost. It was a forlorn, hopeless business. He stalked the country as an increasingly isolated and pathetic figure, addressing audiences of any who would listen to him, while Mrs O'Shea, whom he married in June 1891 after the divorce, sat at home in Brighton. Exhaustion, despair and exposure to frequent drenchings as he spoke to tiny audiences under the open sky took their toll with indecent haste. He died at the age of forty-five, just a few months after his wedding.

In his house at Avondale the human reality of Charles Stewart Parnell comes across in all its poignancy. His portrait shows the emotional intensity, fine sensitivity and keen intelligence of the man who had so identified with the Irish cause as to espouse it in an almost literal sense. The personification of Ireland as a woman, according to Parnell, had much to do with the sacrifices men were prepared to make for her sake. As for his love for Katherine O'Shea, there can be no doubting his ardent devotion, which he expressed in his letters to her. But the nature of Parnell's end seems to suggest that his primary obligation was to Ireland rather to Katherine. For why else would he have driven himself to an early grave, when all practical hope for his political future was gone?

Gladstone battled on with his second Home Rule bill once more in 1893, but the House of Lords predictably threw it out by an overwhelming majority of 419 to 41. Gladstone said by way of a political epitaph to Parnell that 'if these divorce proceedings had not taken place there would be a parliament in Ireland today'. But given the implacable hostility of the House of Lords, it is hard to see how that could have been brought about without amending the British constitution. Between them Parnell and Gladstone did manage largely to resolve the land question that had always bedevilled Ireland. The final step was Wyndham's Act of 1903 which promoted the purchase of

Parnell's memorial in central Dublin spells out in dramatic fashion an article of political faith.

Padraig Pearse's cottage at Rosmuck, Co. Galway, recalls peaceful summers prior to the Easter Rising of 1916.

At Rosmuck on the south-facing coast of County Galway stands the three-room cottage where the militant patriot Padraig Pearse spent his summers. Pearse represented a curiously Irish blend of political idealism combined with a poetic mysticism. He was a teacher whose revolutionary zeal was fused with a heroic vision of the Celtic past. At St Enda's, the Dublin school he founded in 1908, there was a fresco portraying the youthful warrior Cuchulain with the motto in Irish: 'I care not if my life has only the span of a night and a day if my deeds be spoken of by the men of Ireland.' The writings of Padraig Pearse occasionally reveal an instinctive belief that the sacrifice of human life was virtually a pre-condition for the achievement of liberty. 'Bloodshed is a cleansing and a sanctifying thing . . . and the nation which regards it as the final horror has lost its manhood.'

It would seem that Pearse and the other participants in the disastrous Easter Rising of 1916 went about the business of armed insurrection with the deepest conviction that theirs ultimately was the blood that would be spilled. There was thus a heroic dimension to the practical folly of what they undertook when a group of rebels, only lightly armed, set up their defiant battle HQ in the GPO Building in Sackville (now O'Connell) Street. It was Padraig Pearse who stood on the lowest step beneath the imposing Neo-Classical portico to read out the Proclamation of the Irish Republic to a bemused gathering of passers-by. The small band of the self-styled Irish Citizen Army then barricaded itself in its provisional seat of government and awaited the inevitable assault by the British Army. It was to be martyrdom by any other name in the unequal battle of artillery versus rifles and pistols.

Among the combatants was the unlikely figure of Countess Constance Markievicz (née Gore-Booth), once a favourite daughter of the Protestant Ascendancy. In order to visualize and comprehend the enormity of the political

holdings by their tenants and created a new class of small farmers owning their own land. Cynics called this policy 'killing Home Rule by kindness'. But if that was really the hope, then it was a false one; for not only did the Home Rule issue not go away, but it became ever more strident and violent in its campaigns.

By the end of the century there were no longer any single great leaders such as O'Connell and Parnell to unify public opinion behind a united banner. Nationalist movements were fragmented and run by committees of activists. Dublin was a political hotbed of ideas and organizations. But to uncover the traces of two of the most colourful and enigmatic protagonists of the early years of the twentieth century in Irish politics we must travel to two remote locations on the rugged west coast of Ireland.

conversion undergone by this most spirited lady, it suffices to visit her family home of Lissadell in County Sligo. The Georgian mansion was built in the 1830s on lands acquired by the English soldier Paul Gore in the late sixteenth century, who was made a baronet of Ireland in 1621. It was a long and winding road along which this aristocratic beauty travelled before she finally came to take up arms against the interests of her own privileged class. She even denounced her ancestry towards the end of her life as 'that bad black drop of English blood in me'. The route of her political awakening led via bohemian *fin-de-siècle* Paris to the revolutionary circles of Dublin after a conventional launching in society when she was presented as a débutante to Queen Victoria and invited as a guest to the Viceregal Lodge in Phoenix Park. It is strange to reflect on the serpentine paths of human destiny as one surveys the family mementoes at Lissadell. Here, in the elegant drawing-room Constance and her sister Eva made the acquaintance of the poet William Butler Yeats, whose poem in memory of the Gore-Booth sisters is mounted in a gilt frame. Here it was, also at Lissadell, that a ravishing portrait of Constance was made, showing her in a formal gown with train in an almost regal posture, expressing the epitome of Edwardian opulence. With this image in mind let us imagine Constance Markievicz emerging gaunt, dishevelled, dusty and battle-weary from the College of Surgeons in Dublin, where she received the order from Padraig Pearse and James Connolly to make an unconditional surrender.

For the ringleaders of the Easter Rising of 1916 Kilmainham Jail was the next, and in most cases the final stop. This forbidding building on the western outskirts of Dublin had earned a grim reputation since its construction between 1787 to 1796 as the Bastille of Ireland. So many were those rebels committed to serve sentences behind its towering walls that it rapidly acquired the status of a

The drawing-room at Lissadell, Co. Sligo, must have witnessed much of the anguished debate over Ireland's future.

In Memory of Eva Gore-Booth and Con Markiewicz

The light of evening, Lissadell,
Great windows open to the south,
Two girls in silk kimonos, both
Beautiful, one a gazelle.
But a raving autumn shears
Blossom from the summer's wreath;
The older is condemned to death,
Pardoned, drags out lonely years
Conspiring among the ignorant.
I know not what the younger dreams—
Some vague Utopia — and she seems,
When withered old and skeleton-gaunt,
An image of such politics.
Many a time I think to seek
One or the other out and speak
Of that old Georgian mansion, mix
Pictures of the mind, recall
That table and the talk of youth,
Two girls in silk kimonos, both
Beautiful, one a gazelle.
Dear shadows, now you know it all,
All the folly of a fight
With a common wrong or right.
The innocent and the beautiful
Have no enemy but time;
Arise and bid me strike a match
And strike another till time catch;
Should the conflagration climb,
Run till all the sages know.
We the great gazebo built,
They convicted us of guilt;
Bid me strike a match and blow.

October 1927

The famous poem by W.B. Yeats to the Gore-Booth sisters has been copied and framed at Lissadell which inspired it.

political symbol. To do time in Kilmainham conferred a badge of honour; and to be executed there signified a heroic martyrdom. Robert Emmet was one of the first to pass through Kilmainham Jail after his hopeless attempt at insurrection in 1803, though he actually died on the scaffold in Thomas Street. Emmet's speech from the dock showed the way for many others who gave their lives, as it turned out, for no more than the opportunity to broadcast a stirring message that would survive their deaths. Emmet's words became enshrined in popular memory: 'When my country takes her place among the nations of the earth, then and not till then let my epitaph be written.' Robert Emmet became a nineteenth-century folk hero, 'the darlin' of Erin', in the ballad ending 'I lay down my life for the Emerald Isle.'

Parnell had a better time of it than most in Kilmainham Jail during his brief imprisonment of 1881–2. He was lodged in the best available accommodation where he received a flow of visitors and conducted negotiations with the British government in London to conclude what became known as the Kilmainham Treaty, whereby Gladstone agreed *inter alia* to amend the Land Act to give extra protection to tenants who had fallen on hard times. It was even rumoured that Parnell had his own duplicate keys to come and go as he pleased during his six-month incarceration. On 2 May 1882 he emerged triumphant, one of the few members of the Kilmainham club to profit from the experience.

Then in 1883 Kilmainham opened its doors to receive the Invincibles, twenty-six in total, who were accused of complicity in the assassination of Lord Frederick Cavendish and of T. H. Burke within sight of the Viceregal Lodge. The so-called 'Phoenix Park murders' scandalized public opinion in Britain; and a blood retribution was required. Five of the Invincibles were hanged at Kilmainham, and their bodies placed in an unmarked grave by the south-west corner of the perimeter wall. The story of young Tim Kelly, who spent his last night singing all the songs he could remember, concluding with 'There is a Flower that Bloometh', has become part of the Kilmainham legend.

The Easter Rising of 1916 brought a fresh consignment to endure the rigours of the Kilmainham regime. All the signatories of the Proclamation of the Irish Republic and

The grim architecture of penal confinement has been powerfully preserved behind the walls of Kilmainham Jail, Dublin.

most of the other leaders were shot in the stone-breaking yard. The volley of the firing squad was heard at dawn on several days by Constance Markievicz in her cell. Although condemned to death, she was spared by virtue of her womanhood and was later released to become the first elected woman MP in the British House of Commons, but she never took up her seat. A year after the Easter Rising she wrote a verse:

Kilmainham Jail's main entrance appears symbolically to keep the outside world and all its concerns firmly at bay.

Dead hearts, dead dreams, dead days of ecstasy
Can you not live again?
Nay, for we never died.'

The last person to be confined in Kilmainham Jail was the future Irish President Eamon De Valera in 1923–4, but by an ironic quirk of history he was a prisoner not of the British but of the Irish Free State following the bloody Civil War which broke out after the partition of Ireland.

Then all fell silent at Kilmainham. The forbidding entrance gate showing the demons of crime restrained by the chains of law and justice remained shut; and the jail of bitter memories was left to brood on them for several decades. The slow process of natural decay began to undo the physical structure. Rain penetrated the roof, and the moisture rotted the beams and the floors. Sean O'Casey had visited Kilmainham as a young boy in the year 1890 or thereabouts in the company of his uncle. He later described the experience: 'A city of cells. A place where silence is a piercing wail, where discipline is an urgent order from heaven; where a word of goodwill is as far away as the right hand of God; where the wildest wind never blows a withered leaf over the wall.' Very soon after the abandonment of Kilmainham Jail to the elements the place was full of leaves from the shrubs and trees which had established a foothold in this hard world of stone walls.

It was a citizens' initiative which led in 1960 to the launching of a renovation programme at Kilmainham Jail, to create not a ghoulish showcase but a serious museum and above all a memorial to all those who had suffered and died there. It now serves both as a dramatic history lesson in those recent events of Irish history and as a commemoration of the individuals who played their part. Some of their names have been mounted on plaques above the cell doors; and the chapel where Joseph

Plunkett, one of the men of 1916, was married to Grace Gifford just a few hours before his execution, has been re-roofed and restored to mark this final romantic scene of a tragic story.

There are other monuments in Dublin and scattered throughout Ireland, many tended by the National Graves Association, to keep alive the memory of patriots and martyrs. At the north-east corner of St Stephen's Green in the heart of Georgian Dublin there stands a larger-than-life bronze statue of Wolfe Tone, who marked the beginning of a long line of people who were ready to make the ultimate sacrifice. Tone was a radical and a revolutionary, but his vision of a harmonious united purpose across the sectarian divide still has a relevance today. At Glasnevin Cemetery in the northern suburbs of Dublin the greatest concentration of nationalist graves are to be found in what amounts to an Irish Valhalla clustered round the memorial to Daniel O'Connell. But there is a haunting incongruity that hangs somewhere between the resounding words carved on the headstones and the absolute deathly silence of the graves. Glasnevin also contains the graves of some of the many Irish of all faiths who fought together on the same side for the wider cause of the liberty of small nations during the Great War. It is a ghostly ambivalence which serves to remind us above all to tread lightly and with respect as we travel through Ireland, where the past is always close to the surface of the present.

A modern statue of Wolfe Tone has been set up at a corner of St Stephen's Green in central Dublin.

A donkey on the Aran island of Inishmore – no longer such a frequent sight nowadays in rural Ireland.

A SELECTION OF PLACES TO VISIT

County Antrim
Antrim Round Tower
Belfast City Centre
Carrickfergus Castle and Church
Dunluce Castle
Fair Head Crannog
Giant's Causeway

County Armagh
Armagh Cathedrals and Friary
Ardress House
Navan Fort

County Carlow
Browne's Hill Dolmen
Carlow Castle

County Cavan
Drumlane Round Tower

County Clare
Aillwee Cave
Bunratty Castle
Craggaunowen Project
Cratloe Woods House
Corcomroe Abbey
Dysert O'Dea Cross
Ennis Friary
Gleninsheen Wedge-Tomb
Kilfenora Cathedral and Crosses
Killaloe Cathedral
Knappogue Castle
Leamaneh Castle
Poulnabrone Dolmen
Quin Abbey

County Cork
Bantry House
Blarney Castle and House
Cork City Centre
Drombeg Stone Circle
Dunkathel House
Fota House
Kanturk Castle
Kinsale – Charles Fort
Labbacallee Wedge-Tomb
Riverstown House
Timoleague Castle Gardens
Youghal – St Mary's Church

County Derry (Londonderry)
Derry City Walls
Downhill Castle and Mussenden Temple
Dungiven Priory
Mount Sandel Mesolithic Site
Springhill

County Donegal
The Bawn
Doe Castle
Donegal Castle
Fahan Mura Cross Slab
Glenveagh Castle
Glencolumbkille
Grianán of Aileach
Kilclooney Dolmen
Lough Derg

County Down
Ballynoe Stone Circle
Castle Ward
Drumena Cashel
Downpatrick – Down Cathedral
Dundrum Castle
Grey Abbey
Hillsborough Fort
Inch Abbey
Kilclief Castle
Kilfeaghan Dolmen
Legananny Dolmen
Mount Stewart House
Narrow Water Castle
Nendrum Monastic Site
Rowallane Garden
Struell Wells
Ulster Folk and Transport Museum

County Dublin
Dublin City Centre
James Joyce Tower
Kilmainham Gaol
Kilmainham Royal Hospital
Marino Casino
Malahide Castle
Newbridge House
Swords Castle

County Fermanagh
Boa Island
Castle Balfour
Castle Coole
Devenish Island
Drumskinny Stone Circle
Enniskillen Castle
Florence Court
Monea Castle
Tully Castle
White Island

County Galway
Aughnanure Castle
Dun Aengus, Aran
Dunguaire Castle
Clonfert Cathedral
Galway City Centre
Glinsk Castle
Kilconnell Friary
Kilmacduagh Round Tower
Knockmoy Abbey
Kylemore Abbey
Pearse's Cottage
Portumna Castle
Ross Errilly Friary
Thoor Ballylee
Tuam Cathedral and Cross
Turoe Stone

County Kerry
Ardfert Cathedral and Friary
Carrigafoyle Castle
Derrynane
Gallarus Oratory
Kilmalkedar Church
Muckross House and Friary
Skellig Michael
Staigue Fort

County Kildare
Castletown House
Dun Aillinne
Jigginstown House
Kildare Cathedral and Round
  Tower
Moone Cross
Punchestown Standing Stone

County Kilkenny
Dunmore Cave
Graiguenamanagh Abbey
Jerpoint Abbey
Kells Priory
Kilfane, Cantwell Effigy
Kilkenny Castle, Cathedral,
  Rothe House

County Laois
Dunamase Castle
Emo Court
Timahoe Round Tower

County Leitrim
Creevelea Abbey
Park's Castle

County Limerick
Adare Castle and Friaries
Askeaton Castle and Friary
Castle Matrix

Glin Castle
Lough Gur Interpretative
  Centre
Limerick Cathedral and Castle
Monasterananagh Abbey

County Longford
Carrigglas Manor
Granard Motte

County Louth
Carlingford – King John's
  Castle
Drogheda – Town Gate and
  Walls
Mellifont Abbey
Monasterboice Round Tower
  and Crosses
Proleek Dolmen
St Mochta's House

County Mayo
Ashford Castle
Ballintubber Abbey
Croagh Patrick
Moyne Friary
Rosserk Friary
Strade Friary
Westport House

County Meath
Bective Abbey
Donaghmore Round Tower
Donore Castle
Duleek Priory and Crosses
Fourknocks Passage Grave
Hill of Tara
Kells Round Tower and
  Crosses
Newgrange Passage Grave
Slieve na Calliagh Passage
  Graves

Slane Castle and Friary
Trim Castle

County Monaghan
Monaghan City Centre

County Offaly
Birr Castle Demesne
Clonmacnoise Monastic Site
  and Crosses
Durrow Cross
Clonony Castle

County Roscommon
Ballintober Castle
Boyle Abbey
Castlestrange Stone
Clonalis House
Roscommon Castle and Friary
Strokestown Park House

County Sligo
Carrowkeel Passage Graves
Carrowmore Megalithic
  Cemetery
Creevykeel Court Cairn
Drumcliffe Cross
Lissadell House
Sligo Abbey

County Tipperary
Ahenny Crosses
Athassel Priory
Burncourt Castle
Cahir Castle
Carrick-on-Suir Castle
Holycross Abbey
Hore Abbey
Kilcooly Abbey
Knockgraffon Motte
Rock of Cashel

Roscrea Castle, Cross, Round
  Tower
St Patrick's Well

County Tyrone
Ardboe Cross
Beaghmore Stone Circles
Donaghmore Cross
Castle Caulfield
Gray's Printing Press, Strabane
Ulster-American Folk Park
Ulster History Park
Wellbrook Beetling Mill

County Waterford
Ardmore Round Tower
Lismore Castle
Waterford City Centre

County Westmeath
Fore Abbey
Tullynally Castle
Ushnagh

County Wexford
Dunbrody Abbey
Enniscorthy Castle
Irish National Heritage Park
Johnstown Castle Demesne
Tintern Abbey
Wexford City Centre

County Wicklow
Avondale House
Baltinglass Abbey
Glendalough Monastic Site
Kilruddery House
Piper's Stones
Powerscourt
Russborough House

Prehistoric Ireland (until AD 500)

Legend:
- ● Chambered Tomb
- □ Dolmen
- ⬭ Fort
- ✕ Settlement Site
- ⊙ Standing stone or Circle
- ⬗ Royal Mound
- ▽ Other Feature
- – – – Borders of the Five Ancient Provinces

Lough Swilly

Lough Foyle

✕ Rathlin Island

Giant's Causeway

Fair Head Crannog

Mt. Sandel Mesolithic Site

ULSTER

The Bawn

Grianán of Aileach

Kilclooney

Drumskinny

Beaghmore

Lough Neagh

Strangford Lough

Creevykeel Court Cairn

Boa Is.

L. Erne

Ulster History Park

Ballynoe

Carrowmore Megalithic Cemetery

Navan Fort (Emain Macha)

Drumena Cashel

Legananny

Carrowkeel Passage-Graves

Proleek

Kilfeaghan

Slieve na Calliagh Passage-Graves (Loughcrew)

Hill of Slane

Newgrange Passage Grave

Knowth

Dowth

CONNACHT

Cruachan

Castlestrange

Lough Ree

Ushnagh

Boyne

Tara Hill

Fourknocks Passage Grave

MEATH

Turoe Stone

Inishmore Dun Aengus Aran Islands

Aillwee Cave

Dun Aillinne

Punchestown

Piper's Stones

Gleninsheen Wedge-Tomb

Lough Derg

Craggaunowen Project

Browne's Hill

LEINSTER

Poulnabrone

River Shannon

R. Shannon

Barrow

Magh Adhair

Dunmore Cave

Lough Gur Interpretative Centre

Rock of Cashel

Irish National Heritage Park

Labbacallee Wedge-Tomb

Blackwater

Dingle Bay

Bride

Lee

Suir

MUNSTER

Staigue Fort

Drombeg

Bantry Bay

0   40 miles
0   80 km

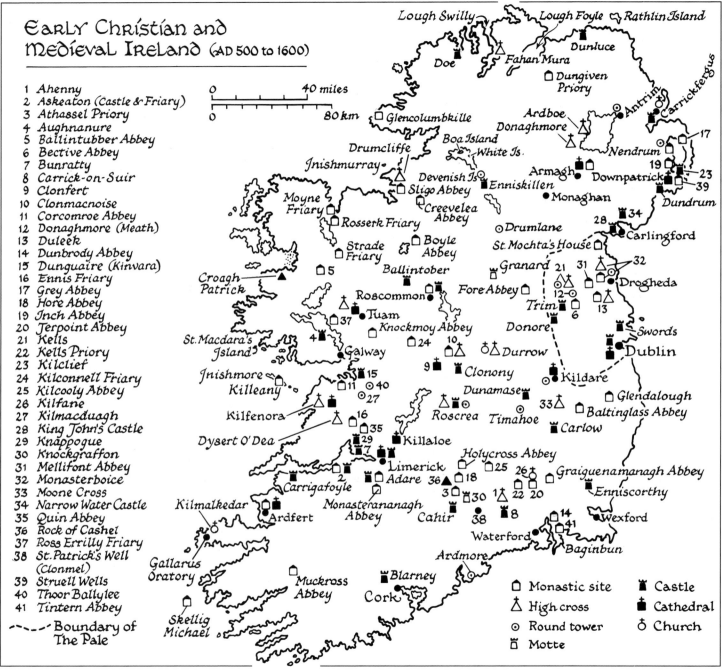

Early Christian and Medieval Ireland (AD 500 to 1600)

1 Ahenny
2 Askeaton (Castle & Friary)
3 Athassel Priory
4 Aughnanure
5 Ballintubber Abbey
6 Bective Abbey
7 Bunratty
8 Carrick-on-Suir
9 Clonfert
10 Clonmacnoise
11 Corcomroe Abbey
12 Donaghmore (Meath)
13 Duleek
14 Dunbrody Abbey
15 Dunguaire (Kinvara)
16 Ennis Friary
17 Grey Abbey
18 Hore Abbey
19 Inch Abbey
20 Jerpoint Abbey
21 Kells
22 Kells Priory
23 Kilclief
24 Kilconnell Friary
25 Kilcooly Abbey
26 Kilfane
27 Kilmacduagh
28 King John's Castle
29 Knappogue
30 Knockgraffon
31 Mellifont Abbey
32 Monasterboice
33 Moone Cross
34 Narrow Water Castle
35 Quin Abbey
36 Rock of Cashel
37 Ross Errilly Friary
38 St. Patrick's Well (Clonmel)
39 Struell Wells
40 Thoor Ballylee
41 Tintern Abbey

----- Boundary of The Pale

0 — 40 miles
0 — 80 km

Lough Swilly
Lough Foyle
Rathlin Island
Dunluce
Doe
Fahan Mura
Dungiven Priory
Antrim
Carrickfergus
Glencolumbkille
Ardboe
Donaghmore
Boa Island
White Is.
Nendrum
Drumcliffe
Inishmurray
Devenish Is.
Armagh
Downpatrick
Sligo Abbey
Enniskillen
Monaghan
Dundrum
Moyne Friary
Creevelea Abbey
Rosserk Friary
Drumlane
Carlingford
Strade Friary
Boyle Abbey
St. Mochta's House
Croagh Patrick
Ballintober
Granard
Roscommon
Fore Abbey
Drogheda
Roscommon
Tuam
Knockmoy Abbey
Trim
Swords
St. Macdara's Island
Galway
Durrow
Donore
Dublin
Clonony
Kildare
Inishmore
Killeany
Dunamase
Glendalough
Kilfenora
Roscrea
Timahoe
Baltinglass Abbey
Dysert O'Dea
Carlow
Killaloe
Holycross Abbey
Limerick
Graiguenamanagh Abbey
Kilmalkedar
Adare
Enniscorthy
Ardfert
Monasteranangh Abbey
Cahir
Wexford
Gallarus Oratory
Waterford
Baginbun
Ardmore
Muckross Abbey
Blarney
Cork
Skellig Michael

⌂ Monastic site
△ High cross
⊙ Round tower
⎕ Motte

▮ Castle
◼ Cathedral
○ Church

232

1 Ardress House
2 Ashford Castle
3 Avondale House
4 Bantry House
5 Birr Castle Demesne
6 Blarney Castle House
7 Burncourt Castle
8 Carrigglas Manor
9 Castle Balfour
10 Castle Caulfield
11 Castle Coole
12 Castle Matrix
13 Castletown House
14 Castle Ward
15 Clonalis House
16 Cratloe Woods House
17 Derrynane
18 Donegal Castle
19 Downhill Castle
   and Mussenden Temple
20 Dunkathel House
21 Emo Court
22 Florence Court
23 Fota House
24 Glencolumbkille
25 Glenveagh Castle
26 Glin Castle
27 Glinsk Castle
28 Gosford Castle
29 Gray's Printing Press
30 Hillsborough Fort
31 James Joyce Tower
32 Tigginstown House
33 Johnstown Castle Demesne
34 Kanturk Castle
35 Kilkenny Castle, Cathedral
   and Rothe House
36 Kilruddery House
37 Kinsale – Charles Fort
38 Kylemore Abbey
39 Leamaneh Castle
40 Lismore Castle
41 Lissadell House
42 Malahide Castle
43 Monea Castle
44 Mount Stewart House
45 Muckross House
46 Narrow Water Castle
47 Newbridge House
48 Park's Castle
49 Pearse's Cottage
50 Portumna Castle
51 Powerscourt
52 Riverstown House
53 Rowallane Gardens
54 Russborough House
55 St. Mary's Church
56 Springhill
57 Slane Castle
58 Strokesdown Park House
59 Timoleague Castle
60 Tully Castle
61 Tullynally Castle
62 Ulster-American Folk Park
63 Ulster Folk and
   Transport Museum
64 Upper Ballinderry
65 Wellbrook Beetling Mill
66 Westport House

Ireland
from 1600 to Independence

233

BIBLIOGRAPHY

Bardon, Jonathan, *Belfast – An Illustrated History*, Blackstaff Press, 1982.

Beckett, J. C. *et al.*, *Belfast – The Making of the City*, Blackstaff Press, 1976.

Bence-Jones, Mark, *Twilight of the Ascendancy*, Constable, 1987. *A Guide to Irish Country Houses*, Constable, 1988.

Craig, Maurice, *The Architecture of Ireland*, Batsford, 1982.

de Breffny, Brian, *Churches and Abbeys in Ireland*, Thames & Hudson, 1976. *Heritage of Ireland*, Weidenfeld & Nicolson, 1980. *Ireland, A Cultural Encyclopedia*, Thames & Hudson, 1983.

de Breffny, Brian, and Ffolliott, Rosemary, *The Houses of Ireland*, Thames & Hudson, 1975.

de Paor, Máire and Liam, *Early Christian Ireland*, Thames & Hudson, 1978.

de Paor, Liam, *Portrait of Ireland*, Rainbow, 1985.

Evans, Rosemary, *The Visitor's Guide to Northern Ireland*, Moorland Publishing Company, 1987.

Fitzgibbon, Constantine, *The Irish in Ireland*, David & Charles, 1983.

Foster, R. F. (ed.), *The Oxford Illustrated History of Ireland*, Oxford University Press, 1989.

Hamlin, Ann, *Historic Monuments of Northern Ireland*, HMSO, 1983.

Harbison, Peter, *Guide to the National Monuments in the Republic of Ireland*, Gill & Macmillan, 1970. *Pre Christian Ireland*, Thames & Hudson, 1988. *The Shell Guide to Ireland* (ed.), Macmillan, 1989.

Harbison, Peter, with Potterton, Homan, and Sheehy, Jeanne, *Irish Art and Architecture*, Thames & Hudson, 1978.

Haverty, Anne, *Constance Markievicz – An Independent Life*, Pandora, 1988.

Lavelle, Des, *Skellig – Island Outpost of Europe*, The O'Brien Press, 1976.

Lehane, Brendan, *The Companion Guide to Ireland*, Collins, 1985.

Loughrey, Patrick (ed.), *The People of Ireland*, Appletree, 1988.

Mitchell, Frank, *The Irish Landscape*, Collins, 1976.

O'Brien, Máire & Conor Cruise, *A Concise History of Ireland*, Thames & Hudson, 1980.

O'Kelly, M. J., *Newgrange*, Thames & Hudson, 1982. *Early Ireland*, Cambridge University Press, 1989.

O'Ríordáin, S. P., *Antiquities of the Irish Countryside*, Methuen, 1979.

O'Síocháin, P. A., *Ireland – A Journey into Lost Time*, Foilsiúcháin Eireann.

Pakenham, Thomas and Valerie, *Dublin – A Traveller's Companion*, Constable, 1988.

Robertson, Ian, *Blue Guide – Ireland*, A. & C. Black, 1987.

Somerset Fry, Peter & Fiona, *A History of Ireland*, Routledge, 1988.

Stalley, Roger, *The Cistercian Monasteries of Ireland*, Yale University Press, 1987.

Weir, Anthony, *Early Ireland – A Field Guide*, Blackstaff Press, 1980.

Woodham-Smith, Cecil, *The Great Hunger*, Hamish Hamilton, 1987.

INDEX